JESUS IN THE MINNOWS

Jesus in the Minnows

—A CATHOLIC BEAT MEMOIR

DAVID CRAIG

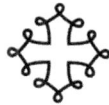

Angelico Press

Acknowledgments

Thanks to two writer friends, Angela (and her VPAA Tom Waits-cranking husband) O'Donnell and Jack Soat, who on the same day two decades or so ago both urged me to write a memoir. I'd also like to thank beta-reader Bill Novak and my dear wife and life editor, Linda, for their support – as well as the ghosts of psilocybin past. And most importantly, I'd like to express my gratitude to Jesus-God, to Pope Francis, and to the gloriously limping Catholic Church.

Laying Your Wet
Hands on the Grass

It's the joke that no one gets, the sunrise that comes
before morning—the Truth delicately awaiting Its
   telling.
Life's just like that, huge answers sitting around,

waiting for the right question, as summer water
waits for the splash of the child. It's our lives as they
   continue
to unfold, the expression of both origin and sway!

Each just far enough in front of us! It's like we get more
of ourselves, the closer we get to our end. Jesus
has divined it so! We are the glorious syllables

of God, Him speaking in tongues. We're the One we
   walk on.
It's why we unroll the carpet of our lives for the people
we meet. It's why those 60s Krishna people

gave flowers away for free (for a time) at the airport,
dressed in those counter-cultural jail-colored robes.
Life is always bringing new ideas—like children's hands

chasing water, a swarm of minnows. You don't need
   to catch them,
your hands marvelously cool and dripping once out.
Should you dry them on your pants or lay them on
   the grass?

Was I the Joint
I'd Been Smoking?

A perfect beauty of sunflower! a perfect excellent
   lovely sunflower exist-
ence! a sweet natural eye to the new hip moon,
   woke up alive and
excited grasping in the sunset shadow sunrise golden
   monthly breeze!
. . . .

Poor dead flower? when did you forget you were a
   flower? when did you
look at your skin and decide you were an important
   dirty old loco-
motive? the ghost of a locomotive? the specter and
   shade of a once
powerful mad American locomotive?

"Sunflower Sutra," Allen Ginsberg

1

You could find me most any morning back then, with Jesus, gratefully tooling down Cleveland's avenues in my wagon full of sunflowers, usually behind a steaming cup of java. What can I say? I liked it, driving taxi, picking up suits, head-bangers, a batch of my forebears under my seat: Merton, Everson & Fabilli, James K. Baxter; maybe some Les Murray or Dan "Stick it to the Man" Berrigan. Langston Hughes. (At that point I didn't know about the Catholic Chilean cudgel, Gabriela Mistral—that singular monster of thwarted love, or about Patrick Kavanagh, the father of spiritual beat poverty.) My fares and I could carry on, talk about whatever we wanted to because in most cases we knew we'd never see each other again.

Plenty of grist for any on-going mill.

Things never start there, though, do they—on nice pink mornings, in a glitter that gently falls from the sky, calling us by our true names? The back of night's two hands has to come first: the loam, the earth, its tangled roots. For me that meant Conurbation, in southeastern Ohio, next to that big river, oil gathering along its futile, crested back, as sad and misshapen a waterway as Cuyahoga's own. At the time, I had just graduated from college and was working for the Federal Government, the Welfare system: a morass of rules, feints, and indirection as far as I could tell, a charitable system whose main function seemed to be to perpetuate itself. (The poor were the tools which made that possible.) The job was a painful excretion, a paper mill. Dickens gone wrong.

The only thing I loathed more than sitting in that padded institutional chair, than being the twelfth successive person to station myself behind that metal desk, was my long-haired boss. The last true bureaucratic functionary, the guy seemed to live for affirmation. For some reason he took a sour shine to me. He'd call me into his office just so he could talk about adjustable-rate mortgages, amortization, deeds of trust. (Why, I don't know, maybe he was trying to save me. The exceptions, the mazes, the minutiae galled — even as the files mounted on my desk.)

His mind was like a small room.

To get away, I'd take to the reservoir at nights, swim, read, smoke some drugs. Womb-water stretched out before me; it was a great place to try to reclaim myself, to remember what I could not, who I was. I loved elementary backstroking my way through moonlight — pulling, kicking, gliding through the dark, rippling the oriental plum sauce: like Li Po in his open boat. It was the breaststroke, upside down, head facing backwards, my life and the progress I almost make: pulling away, moving towards.

You could call it headway, what I could know of that. I liked feeling the slim sheets of muscle as I moved, the shoulder power as I shot along like a slow arrow. I loved the high, dark bowl of stars, the great rims of shaggy trees, the modest cliffs; not a soul around, just white flint, all that possible order above. I liked feeling the sixty percent of me that was water, the claustrophobic breathing, the cooler feel of the depths. Some nights I'd dive and go down as far as I could. I'd have to decide when I had enough air left to make it back up, try to stay a few seconds longer, explode for breath. The whole exercise, tinged with vanity, self-hatred.

An inverted cry for life.

Thankfully, we learn to show ourselves more mercy as we age, as God, who all along has been doing the heavy lifting, begins to get His slow way.

None of that was apparent to me then. I'd read the *Gita*, talked to too many Moses David Christians, some Hari Krishnas. (I read *Allen Verabim* around this time, too, though that might've been a little later.) In any case, I liked to talk about the possibility of God. It was a subject that had always fascinated me. Perhaps I was still that parochial grade school kid, wanting to find out what this life was all about.

Judy would occasionally share my load back then, try to get me to take control of my life. But that would have involved acknowledging some order, that the finality of direction was possible. Still, I liked her, her style, or the lack of it—the trailer park, rodeos, her ruby slippers, vain attempt to yodel when she was in her cups. Sometimes she'd wear one of those long, old dresses, silver-toed boots with no socks. I've have to hoist her last-call swaying butt over my shoulder, deposit her gently, at her own request, into the bed of her pink Ford Bronco. I'd drive home slowly, slide open the rear window just to listen to her singing softly in the back.

Making my way up those reservoir rocks, I'd light up a joint, a small fist against the run-away night, try to write. I'd put some Conway Twitty, Charlie Parker, or Bob Dylan into the 8-track.

Mournful bull roar, most of it, but that was all I had.

As it turned out, both of us quit our jobs on the same day. She'd crocked her grabby boss with an icebreaker. (They used it to try and loosen the glue on the floor beneath the machines at the envelope factory.)

For my part, I never came back from lunch.

She wanted to go to Moorhead or Fargo. "The northern plains," she said. "Picture it: long winters, earned springs."

I just wanted to get away—from the me I had largely constructed.

When we left the bar that night, I took her by the hand at first, walked with her through a star-drenched field of tall grass across the street—until she pulled away. The noises that snapped me back jerked me from my reverie.

6

"Got a toothbrush?" she asked, on her knees.

Barely conscious, she managed to pull out two crates of clothes from her closet before we left her place. Shortly thereafter, she reclined, sawing away, leaning into one of her pillows against the door as we headed northwest in her beat pink Ranger.

". . . the ancient heavenly connection to the starry dynamo in the machinery of the night"?

Sure.

2

With Judy resting along the snores of oblivion, her subwoofers vibrating the bass loudly enough to shake away any pangs of personal regret, I rolled up Route 250, mocking each whining, country-fried, pressed commercial voice as it tried to convince the listener of its ne'er so well-expressed pain.

I chewed gum hard to work against the beer, ate a happy mushroom. Rolling down my window, I let the fast warm air pour in, sang, stupidly as my situation demanded. The trees passed, had their quick say, with the stars and the moon, the spin of all planets. It might have been enough, but I couldn't help wondering what the hell was I doing? My life seemed ridiculous. So it wasn't long before the stuffy summer darkness started to get to me: all the woolen drippings from the fringes of the horizon, my fly-bespeckled life, a combination of sweat and compulsion, a neck that wouldn't set right.

Pulling over, I pitched a few big rocks toward a farmer's corrugated aluminum shed. Couldn't reach it. Too bad. I wanted to hear the metal bend, screech. As it was, all I could smell was cow urine, the warmth and piled blessings of a summer farm night. Nothing like it. I longed in my deepest heart for Roy Acuff, Gene Autry, wanted to set a marshmallowed roll of hay named Reno on fire, just to watch it fry.

None of it brought me home.

I was a black torch in the wind.

We never know what we're doing, where we're going. I, like everybody else, would pass, road kill. Would the stars grieve from their little stables? I stopped again, this time along

8

Tappan Lake: rocks stacked to meet Least Moon Heat's winding blue highway. Taking off my sandals, I waded in, walked the shallows, talked to the moon, that high, thin white thumbnail of concern.

No answers were forthcoming.

Later, standing on the roof of the truck to try and get myself in gear, I shouted at the occasional semi that roared past, Judy tossing beneath me in her personal coma. Bits of passing sand chastised me, one kindly horn. I declaimed what I could remember: what "fuses me unto you now, and pours my meaning into you"?

Behind the wheel, I could feel the fungus start to feed my soil, sang some Brewer and Shipley: "Witchi-tai-to." It made me feel Native. And then in the words of that cracker, Jack (Kerouac): "I bent to it, a-gain," zipped, in my seat, ever northward under the red clover of night, pushing myself until my adrenaline began to merge with the psilocybin.

I would take only no's for answers, pushed past houses, trains, past any sensible need to push. I rode a me that mattered, or seemed to: a guy who was up to something, though I had no idea what that might be.

After about 60 miles or so of that, I found I wanted more than passing trees, sleeping rural houses; so I pulled over for a third time, got out of the pink (or into it), searched the truck bed for a hand spade, then, armed, walked half way into a field. I knelt down and dug vigorously for dirt which I raised up, squeezed into the chalices of my hands. I needed to imbibe the wine of sanctity, find out what it (later) meant to be Quark's hoo-man.

("Bad poetry, Captain.")

I communed beneath the stars with the 'stools, millions of tendrils, fostering good distant trees. I said my name to the popping universe. I was with my sacramental spirit-family: the first ones, the ones who taught matter, plants, God's fibrous nature, what greens us all.

The feel of the gas as it fed itself into the machine fueled me as well. And when, an hour or so later, I saw a sign for Cleveland, I felt as if Judy and I were both part of a larger directive – a sign from the collective second stomach; we must back to the sea. I'd never been to a great lake, after all; to some pretty good ones, sure. But me and the Beev (and Wally), we needed some concurrent action, Mr. Cleever, so I hit the devolution pedal like I had something to prove.

Lights appeared past the last rise heading in. I wanted to feel the liar rise up in me, medicine meeting a lit horizon, like someone out of *The Trickster in West Africa (A Study of Mythic Irony and Sacred Delight)* or Tristan Tzara, Rothenberg in his *Ethnopoetics.* I wanted to wash in the dirt, talk and write like da Vinci – backwards.

Perhaps I could find a niche in this new foreign place.

Carlos Castaneda and his fictionalized anthropological Mexican desert would just have to wait. I would have to try and find what I needed in this particular toucan night.

It would be my feast of burden, my maiden name.

I raced cars so inclined on the freeway, surged past the rails, telephone wires of involvement, past the dead wood in my soul. If there were a reason for my time here, I would have it – between my molars. Like my indigenous buffalo brothers, I would argue with its gristle, feed on its red muscle.

I howled out the window as we flew past the orange barrels, squeezed into the living gullet of urban America. What would be up in this city on the take, on the lake? What was up in the phone wires, in all the hopefully layered voices, playing off of each other? The blue-collared shamans?

I found some Dead Led Zeppelin on the radio, pounded the steering wheel.

Judy briefly moved a leg.

I asked the good spirits to guide me, help me make my bad choices. Grant me un-wisdom, the speech of pelts and cave bones, cold-dark water.

Eventually, I hit the southern edge of the lake, an east-west downtown freeway choice. I chose west because Fargo was in that direction, because it was the way of misadventure, unfulfilled dreams.

I drove like the person I wanted to be, kicked up some shoulder dust, swerving a bit just to stay on point. A turn-off soon appeared for a state park, followed by a sign that said it closed at 11. There were no gates as I inched through the entrance; I could see some Robert Lowell love-cars, hull to hull, parked in their not-right minds.

Striped and painted (like his skunk), I drove slowly down woodsy main, my nose in my cups, leaning over to roll down the lakeside window. I enjoyed hearing the tiny crunch of those gravel skulls as they gave up their ghosts under Judy's tires—as I, an august young Caesar, moved slowly over their compressing mass, until like a front, a living mossy big-lake density impinged.

I smelt the smelt, heard the distant rush of large, indifferent lake waters.

A thick green curtain of heavy air welcomed me, the warm feel of amniotic fluid as I stopped to inhale my origins. I allowed myself to feed off lush lichen, nature's cilia which moved like distant relatives on the rocks, in and out of the water.

I could feel the heaviness of the waves. The constant noise of surf, a kind of invitation; it pleased the animal in me. No one around, I rolled up the windows, locked the truck up, and left Judy in her seat—walked across a huge mown field toward the feeding water, the mouths of St. Anthony's fish.

A few trees, breezes intervened, offering another side of the darkness as I drew closer, their leaves loud and high, somehow completing me—if only for a moment. A chorus, they stood like sentries, or centuries, rustling, no sound of human want in them, speaking foreign tongues, calmly.

They commented on my time left.

It was true. I'd spent too much of my life counting fish, fingers, dancing my almost dance. They spoke earth's longer music. They would remain because they had no time for speech or commerce. All I owned was my quick passing, my scam, my grief. Here the huge cup and moving water, these tall and graceful trees, would rock me to my final sleep – but into my life as well, whatever my deciduous take on things.

All of creation seemed dark praise – death first, yes, with its closure, in those little white bands of surf in the strand to my left; but closer, one small, living wet ride coming in after the other as well. They were a wine that kept offering itself, beauty that was both lance and relief. It kills us because it will outlast us, even as it offers us our spiritual home.

I couldn't take it all in. Canada was out there, grinding its glacial teeth, forever trying to find its (ridiculous) place. No one has yet told them that they don't have one. No country does.

There was a couple off to the far right, talking low, holding hands, their feet testing the water. And closer, two others: family fishermen with lawn chairs and lantern, a cooler. They were a relaxed pair. A pre-adolescent and a step-dad perhaps. The young kid, excited, jabbering away, trying to hook his bait; the older man, silent, enjoying the young boy's enthusiasm. The dad, in his thirties, after some low remark, settled back into the noise his shifting chair made, cigarette dangling, baseball cap.

For him the night was, for the moment, enough, being away, or being here. A cool beer and just the dark clouds he could see out there, the occasional miniature oar boat dimly moving far off in the distance, all the dead Fitzgerald sailors (later), the bend he half waited for in his rod.

What was there to say, really?

And he was right. But for the young one, eleven maybe, he was there with Dad. He had been looking forward to this; you could see that in his movement. This was as close as a young boy gets to his father: the silence between them, in the few words that hook him into ritual, his old man's fleeting graces.

Downtown lights to the far right twinkled, high, out over the water. A different draw.

Farther down the horizon to the left were what looked like suburbs.

Reality! The moneyed.

But why weren't they here? Maybe they had a better view, one that promised chaos, even as they tried to keep it at bay; those couples, safely tucked away – in their constructed art deco compendiums, complete with domestic failure, gin and dubonnets. . . . I long-stepped it over the rocks, reached the edge of the water, enjoyed the rising and sinking, the swell and break of the lake between the shoreline boulders (breaker boulders farther out), the dunking sounds between a few of the nearer rocks as the lake sank then rose between them.

There was a beach to my far left, covered with cool sand which clumped against my now bare feet, altering my gate. Sandals in my hands, I liked the feel of the place – but knew better than to make too much of this. I would have to come back to life when I came down. Maybe we all were just femurs, held up, beating our tune out against the bad teeth of the universe. I could make my hollow noises, but it was clear as I stood there that an occasional reverie was about all I could offer: vague hopes for lost meat, for what I had never possessed. A nostalgia for what I could not name.

Two dead fish at my feet opened their skulls.

Maybe Judy was right.

Maybe there were no answers. Maybe it was just us – molecules and money. Maybe I should go to underwater welding school. Or to the salt mines under this lake.

The sky eventually began to lighten.

(Let me now sing the praises of the Kavanagh.)

3

My nerves began fraying as I started to come down, Judy stirring, puffy-eyed on the far side of the cab. The sky had begun to brighten, rust to red, promising an eventual rise in temperature. I had no idea. Who knew? Maybe something could open up here for us. (My people could finally appear—grandiose, feathered and painted, rising up slowly out of the nearby bushes, speaking my solemn name.)

I greeted her from the floor panel, my back against the door frame.

"Oww, my head. It's coming to one. . . . "

"Squeeze it," I said, tossing her a Coke and a bottle of aspirin. "Smell the water. What do you think?"

"God, I don't know," she said rubbing her face. "Where are we?"

"Cleveland."

"The big city."

"'Just like I pictured it . . . skyscrapers and everything.' . . . Listen to the waves."

I jumped into the seat, queued up some FM. To my surprise, I tuned into the middle of Stevie Wonder's "They Won't Go When I Go."

Odd, and therefore good.

We listened; then she heard it, the sound of water washing in and out, interrupted by the occasional noise whizzing cars made as they passed on the shoreway above. The good damp green smell was still in the air, though it had been tempered some by dew, an early morning mist.

"Let's start a band here."

"You don't play anything. . . . Well, we're not in a hurry. . . . We could look around." At that point, she yawned, got out of the car with a groan, and stumbled onto the field in front of us, scratching her sides for humor's sake.

I followed, walked her down to the rocks to see the water. Massaging her temples, I pumped her with another aspirin, Coke as we kicked our submerged feet, got ready to take on the day—a new lot of (even) strangers.

We ran some along the chilled morning beach, barefooted, just to get our engines started; threw a few rocks, some dead fish into the water, discus style.

Breakfast!

I drove her truck like there was no one else alive through the downtown area, scattering a few of the conventionals in the process. The first promising diner I could find was on the near-east side, on Payne Avenue, a Royal Potato. Three eggs, the window offered in billowed chalk, hash browns and toast for 99 cents. Without pretense, the place had aluminum heating vent ambiance, barely enough room to walk behind one side of the u-shaped counter to get to the least likely stools.

A nice-looking Hispanic waitress named Teresa smiled a gold-toothed smile, stood in front of us on the other side of the counter to take our order. When she actually scratched behind her ear with her pencil, pad in hand, I felt twitterpated.

Judy asked for a local paper, perused the fashion section, want ads.

I went for BD & Doonesbury, the World Series of Rock, sports.

After I'd sopped up the last bit of my home-on-the-range eggs, Judy said she wanted to change clothes, but remembered once we got outside that she hadn't ironed anything. (It was the first time I'd ever heard her use the word!) We left our stuff behind her seat, and walked back toward town, the bigger buildings.

Hand in reluctant hand, we checked out the huge arcades,

store windows, she in her silver-laced boots, torn hem, me with my amen. One of them was a five-story job, a fairyland of old Victorian wood and metal latticework. The roof let in mid-morning sunlight through opaque light green glass. The upper runways were an early morning beehive, buzzing with five and dimes, places that featured late hippy comic books, baseball cards. There was an antiquarian out-of-print book shop establishment—a place for academic re-treads as far as I could see, with fine old wood interior and loosely sweatered owners. Seemed like they were after an aging English aristocratic vibe.

(I pressed my face to the glass! Judy pulled me away.)

There were tee-shirt shops, pipe and fine tobacco places crammed in the smallest of confines, the occasional table out front where tuxedoed violinists tuned up, necks crooked, getting ready for their morning stroll.

It was a pleasant prospect, to sit at the small second tier table and talk, though we felt a little out of place in our pre-owned clothes. Still, once we got beyond that, we enjoyed the soak, the possibilities that always come with new places, mornings. I enjoyed the young male go-fers, the up and coming at you, cups of coffee in hand, jingling keys, change in their off pockets: quick-eyed zuits with tomorrow in their cross hairs.

The whole scene felt like open air, juiced in early sunshine. (Had I a *Wall Street Journal*, and had I known how to do so, I would certainly have creased it neatly, read about important business-related matters.) Instead, I found myself in the opening stages of a huge yawn, chose to wrap myself up in that instead. Large and slow, I uncurled, reveled in each stage like an O'Keeffe desert flower, one petal chasing the others, the smallest of delicate weaves folding back on themselves: all of it done in undulations, in the downside of a dry urban breeze.

It's wonderfully sensual, the luxuriousness one can find in a good yawn. And what else was there to do on a fine morning, anyway, but to indulge, at least for the short time the thing lasted?

That's what they were made for.

I watched as a window dresser changed the jewelry display out front in his store. An old window washer with a huge walrus mustache, farther down to the left, chatted twice with passers-by for every swipe he took at a window. Everyone seemed in good spirits. I liked the descending marbled steps on the other end of the place, spreading out as they gradually did from the initially broad, generous width at the upper Euclid Ave. level to opened arms at the bottom, that level leading to where we had come in, at Superior. The sunlight dazzled in between as it reflected in huge squares off the floors, bounding and then rebounding, like a raining torrent of precious diamonds, a new start right there on the theatrical floor. Those bright corridors, some kind of racial memory, reminded me, in some way, of what I could become.

And, of course, to the trained eye: women! Beautiful young women, each riding the graces of reality, mutual illusion. Tight calves and red spiked heels, red business dresses. Made up to order, whatever their hearts wanted in fine hair, matching lipstick, the calculated flip of the keratin.

None of them tossed in my direction, of course. I looked like seaweed, stewed onions at that point. But that didn't make them less impressive – though the trade-off was more than I've ever wanted to make. Nice clothes and purpose for one window, florescent lights, a coffee man at ten, the scuffle and rut clear to the top, to get there and to stay.

Judy, for her part, seemed more interested. It just wasn't for me. I was fur authenticity, cut speech, a wisp of beard, banjo, barefooted food-stamp kids in patchwork jeans.

I could yodel my poetic lament in high grass. In a Rottweiler neighborhood, a rusted Belvedere with a bad muffler on blocks out front, multi-cultural kids riding their bikes for all they were worth up and down the street, yelling in foreign languages. I wanted two old birds to play rummy with, to cheer for the home team (the Indians – chumps)! More just cost too much, in accouterments, maintenance schedules. The only illusion I wanted was the one that had me going precisely nowhere, in shiny pants, a book of dead-beat poems in my hands to read in a burnt-out hull of an old car at street's end.

That might not be completion, but if it offered hot chocolate once in a while, I figured I'd be jake.

We bought some bagels.

But a big part of Judy was elsewhere. When I inquired, she said she was just real tired of her life, tired of waking up drunk with nothing to show for her efforts but the insides of her stomach.

"Cool," I said. "A thrust, a parry," I recommended hydrotherapy, jai alai.

It took a little doing, but some gratuitous shoplifting brought her around: two small lighters, a top, and the winner: a cheap red functioning plastic whistle (with a raised molded seam)! We decided we liked this new place. There wasn't much pretension—at least until we hit the university some blocks down.

We figured it was the place to go to find housing lists.

I liked those intellectual waif types more than Judy did, all that energy focused on minutiae: on how many answers could dance on the pin of a head. What the heck, one might as well be the hinge, the axle from which all of Western thought swings.

Somebody had to do it.

Judy and I both found a list of possibilities. We'd tried living together, but that lasted four days. There were too many issues: I didn't like her Phil Donahue talk-show topicality, and she couldn't stand being in the same room with a slit-eyed curmudgeon. She'd have friends over, chant from the *Tibetan Book of the Dead* because that's what everybody seemed to be reading just then. They'd beat little drums, tiny cymbals. I, on the other hand, would do too many mushrooms, stack the furniture, or pace the late night roof shingles; I'd go for midnight walks, come back with a sack of snakes, edgy and talkative as a cougar.

She discovered a listing for a place above a store called The Potter's Shelf; some woman who preferred a holistic natural food kind of roommate, someone whose perspective was spiritual, in the Native American sense of that word.

(Sounded like death by cooperation to me.)

I found the right place to hole up until I could figure out how to chew gum and walk at the same time. The Prince Albert (in a can) Hotel, right behind the university. The room was centrally located and cheap; an inside straight as far as I was concerned.

One can per floor.

The rent wrangler seemed nice enough. Americana.

"You ken have a hot plate in your room, but that's off the record cause the state don't allow it. Rent's due on the first. Two days past and yer out. I'll get the po-lice if I need to. Just want to make that clear."

He spoke from over the top of a half-door which separated his office from the vinyl-couched, cheaply paneled reception area where Judy and I stood.

"I have some music I'd like to play up there. Not too loud. That won't be a problem, will it, Mr. Jeffries?" I asked, going with my Eddie Haskell. "A little Hubert Laws' 'Amazing Grace,' Willie Nelson, King Crimson, that kind of thing."

"Willie, you say? No kidding. Why him and I go way back," he said with a smile. "Yeah, I don't know them others, but him and I used to hang out on his porch in the old days, pick some. Course," and here he paused to uncoil a shot of tobacco spit into what I hoped was a cuspidor behind the door, "that was in his outlaw days. Nobody's give 'im a chance in Nashville once he stopped cutting his hair. Guess he had to, how do them hippies say it, find hisself. . . . Found the money basket anyway."

He winked.

"Someone had to."

"Guess that's right. . . . Hey, do you know Hank Williams? My second cousin. Yeah, he was a good un too. Course he was an alcoholic. Which reminds me, no drinking up in those rooms. I hate cleaning up after people. We've had some trouble with that. . . . You interested in a front window? That's all we got."

"Front's fine. So you hung with Hank?" I was amazed.

"Well, I was pretty young at the time. He'd let me strum his guitar when I come over. I was just a sprout." At the point he looked down and stepped on something.

Hearing the thing crack, I cringed. Maybe I was in the wrong can.

But then his better half spoke from behind the nailed red and white checkered shower curtain that separated the three of us from their living quarters. "Get the date right on the damned receipt this time, will you? I cain't keep the records right if you cain't read the damned calendar."

I could hear the soap opera on her TV, imagined her sitting with her fuzzy balled slippered feet propped up on a round vinyl ottoman, the kind with a big, depressed button in the center, sipping a can of Bud in a flowered house dress, a Camel in her off hand.

I liked the place. My soul in macrocosm. What it lacked in style, it more than made up for in élan, inner city urban verité.

"Picky, picky," the man of the house said. "Get out a my face for I lump up yours. . . . Dang women," he said, looking at me. "If you don't set 'em up right, they walk all over you."

I leaned over the door, liked what I saw of his inner sanctum. A blond-grained coffee table sat in the center of the room, and on it, an ashtray stuffed with lip-sticked butts. A velvet Elvis, a good one, graced the kitchen above the table where, soon enough, he took to very carefully forming the letters as he wrote out my receipt on a little tear out page. Even the vinyl-seated chairs in there were vintage: the backs, thin-piped, formed hearts. There was a second, small TV in there on the counter, so she could watch *As the World Turns* as she made tuna salad sandwiches.

Judy ground her teeth

"Shall we at least check out the upstairs before you dive right in?" she asked, rubbing up her bare upper arms.

"Woman, mind your place," I said.

She was not amused.

(Sometimes she was just no fun.)

And soon Jake and I were dutifully climbing the stairs behind her. The stairwell was darker than I had expected, one slightly swaying 60 watt bulb, dark brown paint flaking from the bottom half of the walls, a newer beige on the upper half.

Once we got inside, I asked about the cleaning woman. "Got a bucket and some Lysol downstairs," he answered. The mantle looked as if it might have been green under the dust, and the old fireplace was papered over. The bed sagged. I looked over to Judy who was tapping her foot, scowling, and began to question my choice.

She was probably right. Who knew what was living up that flue? But then, as I did the perfunctory tour, I looked out the window and saw the Greyhound bus terminal down the street—a nice place, it would turn out, for pilgrim dinners.

"I know it's crazy, but I like it," I said. "It has the feel, the grandiose pathos of a life almost lived, a garret. I can brood here, write my painful but evocative symphonies."

She ran a finger across the mantle, looked at the caked dust. "Jim, you don't write." And then, after a pause, "Sometimes I can't believe how self-destructive you are. Do you actually have to seek the gutter? You don't have to make things harder on yourself, you know. Life will do that. You could spend your energies elsewhere."

I found a small Gideon's in the table stand drawer.

"It's a perty nice place, I say," Mr. Jeffries added. "I mean, for the price."

But then he saw Judy's face. "Look, I'll wait downstairs while you two'ns decide. Someone else was askin' about it earlier," he said with a final wave of the hand.

"It's not funny anymore, James. You can do what you want with your life, but don't expect me to be coming over here. I want something better, something tangible."

I tried the window. It opened!

Cool.

"Look at that! . . . If you don't like it, don't come over. That's pretty simple."

Neither of us was sure what was happening between us at the time. We hadn't been sure for a while. So after the frequent rough patch, we'd both usually find ourselves treading water, waiting for things to work themselves out. It was all we had. We'd simply fill our expected car seats, hope for the best.

That's how it felt as we made our way toward Pottersville. She pulled over at a BP near my place, changed clothes, washed up in the bathroom sink. A new top. Nice. And after quietly driving through the largely toothless and poor Chester Ave. corridor, we took Cedar Hill like we were on a mission, came to the Heights.

It looked like a nice area, I said, trying to offer some support. The older residential homes were well kept, as were the older apartment buildings.

It should be safe anyway.

The Potter's Shelf window was a revelation. Hep-cat Indian-looking jugs sat on top of Navajo rugs; hanging beads strung nicely along either side of the book display, featuring the visions of Chief Yellow Apple.

(Oprah before her time.)

We rang the buzzer and were let in, made our way over the tiny black and white floor tiles, Art Deco from the thirties, up some worn-to-a-tough marble steps. An attractive, made-up woman sized us up above the opened door chain, soon putting her hand on each of our shoulders as we walked past her, talking generously all the while. Her name was Liz, and she just knew, hearing Judy's voice over the phone, that she would be the right one.

"Money's not a problem?" She got a "not at all" and so continued. "Well, not to worry. We'll help you land something. I'm a flight attendant, myself. Nothing much of course, but it pays the bills. I am getting a little tired of it, though, to tell you the truth." She touched Judy's arm again, smiling. "It's like being a waitress in a bad restaurant at 30,000 feet if you know what I mean." They both laughed.

"It's a trade-off. That's how I see it. Time given for a trip back home to Puerto Rico every year. . . . " She smiled at me. "I'm thinking of law school, environmental or corporate. I don't know which. What kind of job are you looking for? I can put out some feelers."

4

Within two weeks I was working at a warehouse, while Judy, no surprise, found employment at the pottery shop. My job was atonal, a tough sled. It's a process I've always hated: pushing hard for a job I don't really want because I need the money, trying to look as interested and involved as possible; and then, worst of all, getting the thing, having to show up every day for the grim pellet.

I told the interviewer I'd never finished college, that I'd been hitching around for a few years doing odd jobs: a dude ranch just east of Yellowstone, street-vending in New York, working on a fishing boat right outside of Delacroix. I told the second interviewer about my old granny, my only living relative. (She lived in town.) I needed to settle close to her, help her out in her dotage.

I did like the service industry, though. I told them both that; I felt like the middleman had been undervalued. I complimented the lay of the physical plant, piped in with a few jokes when a lull dictated, figured that they were probably bored with the work, too, and could go for a stable cut-up.

My destiny was basically to fill orders, to haul boxes of Rubber King Jubilee products from different pallets to a conveyor belt. Me and my in-a-few-weeks-to-be pals rode around on the forks of our electric jacks whenever beyond the eyes of our bosses. We'd crash them into brick walls, pillars, each other, just to jar our fillings. We talked the rot young men do when they work dead-end jobs. How much we were going to party, where to buy good drugs, the secretaries who all wanted white-collar guys on the fourth floor.

My soon-to-be partners in crime were named Carp and Donny. Carp was a long haired skinny would-be roué, a wispy-bearded comedian. Riding the rainbow of crystal meth, he seemed to be coming in long after the hippie fact, but that didn't seem to affect his roll. He was from the West Side as it turned out, and that, as I was to learn, accounted for just about everything back in those days. He always wore tight shirts, his bony physique like a badge, trying to convince the girls that he was a rock 'n' roll idol or could have been so had he wanted that.

He was a funny guy, always trying to sell me something hot; he'd take me out to his bomber after work, open the rear door to a full rack of clothes. One time he had banjos for sale, another time huge tool chests. And guns. He said you could never be over-prepared in this day and age.

(He got murdered by a quasi-friend a few years later. Speeding, the two of them, and then an argument over a rotary phone on the kitchen wall.)

Donny was different. (He later drowned, drunk in Lake Erie.) He was an overtly self-destructive kind of guy who would probably rob you once he got to know you well enough to come over to your house. He was everything I wanted to be in my most manic stages. He lived as if he wanted to crash his head into the walls of life, taste the juices – like somebody who couldn't get into Dante's poem.

Ugolino's cousin.

At about five-eleven, he was big, strong, doughy guy, would threaten to tap-dance on Carp's forehead at least three times a day. He was a serious drinker as well, no stranger to speed. He'd come in the morning, wide-eyed, with Mad Dog on his breath, keep a flask of something for a quick tipple. And everybody there was like that to some degree, some gum on him at all times. You could find him between the stacks.

When I first went out with these two guys for lunch, I was surprised to find so many co-workers in front of us at the corner store, each of them there for the bargain grape. Guys would sit in the grass on nice days, as I learned to, lean against the back windowless wall of the building or against telephone poles, cables, brown-bagging it.

It looked like wino heaven, a purgatory run-up.

Donny's van was brown with a purple interior. Just the two seats up front, purple plush carpet in the back, these little round skulls that hung all the way around the edges of the van's ceiling. Donny and Carp, a couple of Kurtzes, but funnier.

"No man, give me the wine. No, to me," Carp would say to Donny, though he had the bottle and no one was asking for it. He'd push imaginary intruders away.

"Shit, man, give it up. Buy your own," Donny would answer, taking Carp's for a deep swig.

"Don't give me that shit, man. I bought last week, and the week before."

"Yeah, but you owed me."

"Owed you? For what?"

"Give me a second," Donny replied as he finished half of what was left. "Okay, who's got the reef?" he asked, moving his head all around in his manic way.

I tossed a bag up from the back. Both looked at each other, smiled.

"Hey, man, you ought to come out with us to Barry's this weekend. We could do some target practice." With that Carp pulled a .38 from the glove compartment, tossed it back to me. I was surprised, taken aback.

The thing was heavier than I expected. Ash black, with a nice, brown-grained handle.

"You guys ever use this?" I asked, aiming it out the window.

"Gimme that," Donny said. He got out of the driver's seat, took it, and walked to the main street where he emptied the chamber into a quickly swaying stop sign.

"Clint Eastwood," Carp said from his seat. "Give the guy a gun and right away he's a bad ass."

"N-gger adjusted," Donny said, getting back into his seat. The guy never looked comfortable; he sometimes seemed like he could hardly contain his own energy, as if he felt stifled within the confines of his skin. Like he had – or was – a tick.

God rest our (disturbed) souls.

They picked me up early on July third, and soon we were barreling east on 90, heading for Conneaut, twelve cases of Miller High Life on board, much of it rattling uncomfortably over and against my back. I managed to create the only stability I would know by lying back, keeping the cases away with extended legs. Hard to drink that way, but I managed.

When I asked them how they'd rounded up so much, they looked at me as if I were from another planet. Forklift. (They'd busted into a box car, had subsequently stashed cases all over the mid-west side.)

Barry's place was off an unpaved country road. We were so stoned by the time we got to that neck of the woods that we passed up the entrance twice. Eventually we found it, though, and as we pulled up the long, sorry, muddy drive, I thought of the movie *Deliverance*, began squealing like a pig. Carp soon joined me, both of us snorting and truffling for answers, ready, as my grade schoolteachers would have put it, to act out.

This was clearly going to be a real exercise in futility.

The two of us rocked the van from side to side for all we were worth, me trying to break the fall of tumbling cases with my hands and feet at the same time. We got the rise we wanted out of Donny. He tried to reach over and slug us as he drove slowly, told us he'd shoot us if we tipped him.

But we dodged him easily enough: "It's his fault."

"No, no. It's his, It's his . . . Mom! Mom!"

The trailer, "Farther," came into view, and that put an end to our carrying-on.

Donny slammed on the brakes, told us to get the hell out.

Carp responded by shutting the door harder than he had to, told Donny to walk home then.

The sorriest white aluminum Smaug I'd ever seen, before or since, stood there on three stacks of concrete blocks, the middle stack, beginning to crumble. The thing looked like an old swayback, with a flat rock step, too far down, below the side front door. A big black peace sign had been painted under a window to the left along with some gang letters and a family of small stick people, the man with a large red penis.

There was a circular ash heap to the right of the door like some ring of passage, surrounded by folding chairs, one large old, padded rocker, and a long console TV cabinet plugged in with an orange industrial strength extension cord strung through a lifted window. The place did have ambiance, you had to give it that: a picnic table off to the left, a cupped satellite dish with a Mr. Hero sandwich and a huge, uprooted weed resting in the center.

A place to self-actualize.

The whole tract of land seemed to have been a swamp at one time as there were traces of puddles all around, even though it hadn't rained in a week. Mosquitoes were out in force; a big net, apparently in place for just such eventualities, had been rolled up and tied with ropes against the trailer roof. Swatting bugs, I wondered what it would take to bring that mesh down.

My rueful musings were interrupted, however, by laughter coming our way through the trees, young women among the group. (Perhaps I had missed the true spirit and value of this place?)

I wasn't surprised when I noticed that Donny had initially left the beer inside the pulled-up van. There was already some on ice next to the big chair, and it would have taken a while to get the new brew cold. But when I saw the two of them pull out what looked like semi-automatic rifles which had been stashed behind the local beer, my anxiety level did rise some.

Barry, the owner of the property, another guy, and two girls walked around the front of the van. Barry was hugely affable, especially after I handed him an ounce of Cambodian. Like Carp, he had that wispy bearded look. The Eat Possum hat and barrel chested girth were, however, his own touches. "How ya doing?" he asked shaking my hand. "Welcome to the quake near the lake. We gonna partee," he said to me, turning immediately to respond to one of the girls who had said something about his trailer.

He was a goodhearted, expansive master of ceremonies, in a brown plaid lumberjack shirt, frayed at the cut-off sleeves. Built like a truck driver in his blue work pants, he wore boots big enough to stomp the firma. He greeted Donny and Carp with fake bump hugs, hearty complicated handshakes, told us to help ourselves to the liquor under the sink.

The nice-looking girls, Monique and Spot (she, too, sadly, having recently passed) seemed younger than it turned out they were, probably due to the fact that they were always tittering. They both had the look of mid-westside women, with long straight hair, though Spot's, which was naturally light brown, had a graceful trace of wave at the end. Monique's was peroxide blond, straight and coarse, which she maintained by careful and constant combing. She came across immediately as a cut-up. But the mascara and thickly clumped lashes made her seem, perhaps, a slightly sad case, set off as they were against her pale complexion, her stubborn pink rouge.

Both had nice little figures, wore snug jeans, dark and pale tops: Spot with a tan pullover, just loosely fitting enough, a tee shirt actually, with the beginnings of a low cut, and Monique, a white, short-sleeved kind of fuzzy thing with bits of turquoise jewelry sewn in.

We all quickly introduced ourselves and went inside to escape the late morning bugs, to crack open a few and talk about concerts, work, drugs. The important things. There was an old fridge in there that spoke in rattling bottles whenever you opened it, four large bowls of cleaned weed on several coffee tables in front of an old couch. Another on the old kitchen counter, what there was left of that. The Formica had long since gone the way of all flesh, and all that was left was wet plywood, in splinters underneath, that and the glass-less window behind, faded yellow curtains blowing in and out.

I scooted an abandoned old black vinyl front car seat over toward the couch. Better access to the pot. Those more comfortable with the place, Donny and Carp specifically, man-spread, took up most of the couch, began to fire up the pipes. The girls joined in, pulled up a few kitchen chairs.

"Man, I been waitin' all week for this," Carp said.

"Is that why you didn't do any work?" Donny responded.

"Boys, boys," said Spot. "Calm down . . . and pass that bowl." She laughed, liking the sound of it: the mirth she had created.

"Hey, no probleemo," Barry said, coming over with beers; he lit up two pregnant joints, passed them around in the opposite direction. "Nobody gets out of here alive." Everyone who could, laughed. (All the strained sucking, blowing, coughing. It sounded like we were all under tents in an intensive care ward.) "You from around here?" Barry asked me in a higher voice.

"Na," I said, talking that kind of higher-pitched kind of talk people do when they try to hold in a lung full of smoke. "Ohio River—though I do hate Pittsburgh."

He and the girls laughed.

"Works with us, the loafer," Donny threw in.

"Sucks up to the boss and then goes up on the fifth floor, hides in the stacks. Like we don't know or something," Carp added.

I coughed. Thought I had been sneaky about that.

"Hey, come on. I'm just trying to fit in."

"He brings dope, though. So we talk to him," Donny added, exhaling.

"What do you usually do on weekends?" Monique asked me. "You surely don't hang out with these guys all the time, do you?"

Oohs went up.

"Ah, not too much. I came up with a woman, but we're kind of on the outs. . . . I want to meet some poets, though. Brought some bongos. They're in the truck. What do you think? We could recite. I've got a couple of berets, a few chapbooks. We could be authentic or something like that." Not a good idea: bringing up something depressing – and poetry.

The place got quiet for a moment.

Spot saved me, reinflating the ball and putting it back in play.

"I want to go out on the lake next weekend. Is your boat fixed yet?"

"Yes, your majesty," Barry said. "Would you like us to send the car around?"

"That would be nice."

"Gosh, why doesn't someone clean this place?" she asked.

Barry burst out laughing, shook his head. He walked over to the corner and, turning, tossed her a broom. "Earn your pig, oinker. We've got poets coming over."

"Got any pots?" I said. "We could improvise. Do some large mushrooms . . . we could climb the trees at night, sway up there in the midnight wind like Christmas ornaments, make a statement. Hari-Rama, my brother . . ."

"Never mind. It would take too long," Spot replied to Barry, waving her hand, ignoring my creativity. As other people started to talk about an upcoming concert, I noticed that she was using the stick end of the broom to playfully sweep the webs overhead back and forth, as if they were in a breeze.

We kept passing around the joints, bongs, small pipes in different directions as conversation began to splinter, permutate. All the smoke hung over us like white paternal hands, a soft ghostly strata; in sheets, moving now, slowly westward, a pall over the late morning moors, the Scottish highlands with their kilts and obscene pipes, their dank foreign languages, guttural sounds; a pale haze, covering the land, opaque to reason, the sun's rays. It would have us in the end; it would surround us – wrap us up, a murky membrane.

Cut off from the sun's rays, we would be left alone, in painted faces, holding our Munch ears. . . . Crying out for Gerald Ford, federal assistance.

(I had been talking.)

"Is that poetry?" she asked. "Where do you read, in a closet?"

Barry smiled. "Look, I think they're communicating."

"Let's get this started."

He had to move. It was time, he said, to get the pig going; so he got up, walked over and threw open the screen door the way he probably did on most days, smacking it hard into the vinyl shingles outside, catching it on the rebound as he passed.

The others followed, several of them comically doing the same swing and catch routine.

Spot and I stretched our legs, sat on the floor, me against a wall. We lit another pipe. She told me about herself: dental assistant school, her neighborhood.

"So what about you, poet?"

I told her I was in my semi-annual stasis, pupa stage. . . . I felt like I was in one of those Escher paintings where the stairs can't agree.

"I get it. 65th Street."

A banging outside shifted our attention. We stood by the door and saw Carp, standing on some kneeling guy's back, sledging in a five-foot-high stake. For a turning spit. And down the muddy road, Donny and three other guys I hadn't seen before running toward us with a good-sized pig on a metal rod, a beer can in its mouth. Barry, meanwhile, walked out of the woods with a stack of firewood in his arms, dropped them in a pile. He pulled out a gun from his back black belt, started firing it into the air.

"Party til you puke."

"They do this along the Ohio?" she asked.

"Yeah, but we have to hunt down the pig first. Boars. Big-assed. With Bowie knives, you know? Slit their throats like I seen 'em do in New Zealand and Texas. . . . *Let it Bleed.*"

Football exhibition season had just started, so Barry and a few of his buds pulled up chairs as we waited. Before long, a

crowd of eight or so people had joined in, all of them cursing the owner, Art Modell. One of the new long-haired guys,
Arnold (Carp's brother), kidded Spot about one player's tight
end, using a dumb-ass pseudo-space cadet inflection. Later, he
shook my hand, introduced himself as the strawberry blond
Rasta Mon.

"Is there a union or something? For poets, I mean," he asked.

"We should start one. I'll collect the dues."

"You won't get much, I'll bet."

"Pig's on," Spot eventually yelled. "And no comments while I
have this carving knife." Like a pride of lions, most of us, blade
in hand, descended, took his or her beery chance. I stationed
myself near the high rump and carved away at the ham, gorging
myself with a slab, passing chunks around, yelling for more
ale, some jousting, time-specific revelry.

Barry liked that one.

Spot and I talked, and between my barely audible grunts
and her solid, neat potato salad paper plate, glasses of liquor,
we got on.

One by one, the lions fell to the drier portions of grassy
turf, roaring, licking their scarred faces, paws. I don't know
if it was because the two of us were enjoying our conversation
or because we both just felt contrary, but neither wanted to
flop to the turf. So, I grabbed the bottle of liquor she had been
pouring from, and we headed for the trees.

We got back late in the evening, broke from our hand-holding
as we approached the others. Tents had been thrown up. There
were empty bottles everywhere. I suggested a bonfire to Barry.
We could cross arms, hold hands, sing Kumbaya.

Or Joan Baez—we could heal the forest.

He said I was melted.

Digging quickly around, he found a rolled up sleeping bag
and tossed it to me. We wended our way through the bodies,
found a tent and crashed for the night, just the occasional

sound of owls, people on that well-traveled two-lane gustatory highway behind a stand of bushes to our left.

Morning came, as it often does, too early, though that fact had escaped Carp and Donny; the two of them were wide awake, sitting on creaking lawn chairs, discussing last night's escapades. Tripping, they had bicycled up and down the country roads with rifles across the handlebars, had shot up mailboxes, corn stalks, gone swimming in somebody's pool. When an inside light came on there, apparently, they'd initially yelled for the residents to come out back for a swim.

When they heard the sirens, though, the two of them had to split through the woods, dragging their bikes and rifles behind them. After an hour or so, though, because they were who they were, they went back, took another dip, one of the older kids from the house this time finally coming out to join them.

The dude emerged wearing one of those inflated little kid waist-encircling ducks, invited them both to a party later in the week.

I only caught only bits after that: Puffed Wheat cereal. The mom made eggs and bacon.

As for me, I felt wasted, charred: gargled, a dreg, small, choking in my own fumes. There had been some fun here, but I didn't like the pile of fecal matter I'd become. Some part of me wanted to feel better about myself.

Later, I tried to quiet the birds, squeezed off a few blind rounds in their general direction. The howls and moans rising up from the churning bags, however, moved me to desist.

But how could I?

How could any of us?

We were here for the long haul. To nobody's credit. All of us knew too well our own stench, raged over what was missing in our lives, a need so big it could have argued for Descartes.

Whatever the case, it was clear that we were living our lives as if they didn't matter.

People lay all over the compound, moaning, turning, like some outtake from Waco (later). Human debris, all of us. The young and pointless (a soap!), in a world that offered us exactly nothing.

A car later made doughnuts in the mud, running over spewed saplings, beer bottles on a Sunday morning.

We needed something to get us past us.

My fellow 4H-ers, for their parts, had made it a point of honor not to consider anything beyond the purely physical. Like me, they wanted to run the present moment into the ground, to stomp it until it squealed, died a piggy death. Then, like Mick Jagger, they wanted to scrape those entrails right off of their shoes.

We all knew the price we were paying.

The trouble was, it was the only game in town.

What if Jesus-God were to walk among those bottles, tents (in His authentic Mediterranean garb)? What would He have said?

First of all, I think He would have bent down, lifted up my ground-level visual flap, others' as well. Would He have been outraged? No, I don't think so. I think He would have smiled. He would've said to the younger me, "You're getting closer; you're hearing what I've been saying." (Gideon's.) Maybe He'd have walked around, started picking up all the bottles, adding "What can one give to the dead, the dying, James? . . ." And then, maybe, to the older me: "Take me with you . . . now. . . . I have always had a weakness for the unreal, the fictional, the broken. I am God. That's why I came. I want them all. They are my children. . . . Beat your little drum if you want to."

Order is something I could not bring to the party, something I don't bring often enough now.

"All you can ever be is that quiet, voice."

I think that's what He would've said.

I thought of Him once in a while back then – all those pamphlets the Moses David Jesus people used to pass around back at my college. I never went to any of their meetings. They were clearly after (or on) some happy juice, but that didn't mean there wasn't anything beyond this physical carnage either.

Maybe my grade school biker-nun had planted seeds. Eighth grade. I liked her, despite her stinging ruler against my opened palm (oh worms of pain!). The sisters could be violent – but they did try to love. They had a center; not that progressivist horseshit I'd gotten from the public schools.

The crazed there, in Conneaut, in their way, were showing some courage in the face of the wastage they saw. Judy's kind of people, in that respect anyway; at least until she'd heard the buzz of neon, the rustle of fine silk.

Spot made overtures a little later in the morning, attempted to solidify what had happened the night before between us, asked me if I wanted to walk the frontage road.

Those moments are crucial, what you say or don't, the kind of body language you give. I knew that, but I knew this whole thing was a mistake too.

At first, I didn't answer.

She laughed a slightly strained laugh, went outside, took to brushing her hair briskly, head bent over to one side.

I felt bad about my silence, joined her, offering a beer, a spare pair of shades.

"God, my head hurts. Did we comport ourselves properly last night?" she asked, pulling on the front of her shirt, trying to laugh.

"Well, that would've been a first," I said, taking a swig of beer.

She wrapped herself in her arms for small comfort, laughed, asked which way the road was, though she already knew and had started heading in that direction. "So you want to be a writer? Isn't that what you said?" she asked, walking a step ahead as we made our way up the muddy drive.

"Did I say that? I must've been drunk. . . . Rimbaud sold slaves."

"Who was he?" she asked, laughing. "Probably someone famous I've never heard about. . . . died poor, didn't he?"

"He had a gift."

"Why bother?"

"Maybe it was something in him—like he had to do it. Maybe he wanted to contribute to the betterment of society, find peace on earth, like Miss America."

"I'd rather play tennis. Do you play?"

"I can't. Too much exercise and sun are bad for me. I prefer florescent lighting, Twinkies."

"You can't? You should see me, balls flying over the fence, into moving cars. I had to chase one down the block last time. It beat me to the sewer."

A few more yards down the morning road and she was into the flowers. "What are these called, do you know?"

"Head of the Corpse. . . . God, you're incorrigible, aren't you?"

"I just like flowers. That's a good thing," she said tossing her hair back. "Here, take some aspirin." I could see, for the first time, high across her chest, a lot of tiny, tiny pimple bumps under her nicely tanned skin. She looked good, was pretty even. But there were nerves going on here as well.

"Let's play sometime. It would be fun."

"Wait a minute," I said as I went between a few neighboring trees to retch against the night. Spitting out the last few strings of regret, I decided that I liked her doggedness. More than I liked her, early on.

What the heck, I figured, I didn't have anything going.

I was lonely enough not to want to cut this new tie, so I said just enough to keep her interest. I would be pond scum either way. If I eventually dropped her, I used her; if I didn't, I'd use her the more, dragging out the inevitable. I did like her, just not enough—though lit moonlight candles, incense, and Perry Como music (Universal Man) certainly have never been guarantees of anything either.

We all just kind of walk around, don't we, with our pockets turned inside out?

The tennis experiences had their moments, but they brought the stress of the inevitable. Near the end I just hoped I could keep it going long enough to make it look like I had given it an effort. She lacked something I needed: an IV of self-hatred perhaps, a larger artistic (or autistic) sensibility.

For her part, she was just elsewhere; she wanted what she could get in her life, tried to work within those confines.

She had some courage.

More of her company certainly would not have hurt me.

But I didn't like tennis rackets or fences or nice blue-collar neighborhoods, the trimmed bushes. (They never helped.) The whole scene required more amendment than I was willing to make.

Everybody was up and chugging beers by the time we strolled back into the compound. Standing next to Spot, watching, I could see we were all doing the same thing. We were trying to leech the moment, to suck it bone dry, looking for something sustaining, running from and back to the closest thing we could find to the grim protein slime we had crawled out of, millions of years ago.

"Bill!". . . "Nancy!" (They missed each other!)

I could hear my own voice gurgle as I slipped, unnoticed, back into the vast protein stew, the green foam.

Hitching the 80 or so miles back, I carried on with each person who picked me up like it was old home week: trying to be friendly to the unaware driver, always with a trace of self-mockery.

One guy handed me a JW pamphlet.

As summer moved into fall, I found myself marauding less and less with these jar-heads. Less and less with anyone for that matter. I began to curl inward, to just sit, far inside my opened window, the cooler air coming in, looking out over the skyline. For hours, it seemed. All the evening noises: the cars, the horns, the occasional shout, the crew-cutted ex-Nam vet who used to stand on the sidewalk glass in front of our building, rock back and forth, shouting at his enemies.

I'd listen to my cassettes, went to a few poetry readings around town.

Felt too distant to try to connect.

People farther down the street went in and out of the Grey-hound bus station, all the cabs, the law students with brisk, purposeful walks. Judy and Spot had both faded from the picture, and I just didn't feel like meeting anyone else. I'd go into Plain Dealer bars downtown: funsies at Nunsies, one bar's nose-less proprietor. I'd sit and drink, brood over my stool, alongside reporters who would play pinball, each of us waiting for something large and potentially meaningful to happen in our lives.

I'd talk with people over at Madden's on 13th. Good literary folk, college, once or twice removed – softball types. Played a couple of late games with them. They liked Bukowski, Joyce, J. P. Donlevy, Richard Brautigan. They saw the Beats as posers.

I met a nice young lady there. She wanted to be a grade-school teacher. We talked it up a few times. I couldn't quite wrap my head around her. What was this? Suburban sustain-ability? Intractable optimism? (A good egg nonetheless: June.)

Part of me liked getting drunk, at least the happy walking-out-late part. I could sing under the stars. I'd talk to the occa-sional tree, my stout brother, as I made my way home under the happy dark green, the brick, streetlight.

The soft lap of those leaves, the nostalgia overhead, the eventual clogs of fall humus in the gutters, the curbside rivulets seemed altogether beautiful to me.

The whole drunken scene offered a weird kind of hope as green growth clung in ivy twigs to every wall, around every wire. I took to clambering over barbed-wire fences on my cir-cuitous journeys room-ward, would wake with crabbed and cut hands, a frog in my throat, pieces of my head all over the bed.

I'd eat at least once a week after work at the Greyhound station. Crusted mashed potatoes under those lights. Limp beans, pale under the interrogation, and breaded near-meat. I'd wash it down with a can of Coke. Then I'd go out on the main floor and put quarters in a TV, watch those little sets for an hour or so. Floor wax commercials, life with mortgages, new cars, children, attorneys who could get you money.

I liked them best, thought of trying that. (Real religion there.) The university's law school was just down the street. No curves in the architecture. There had to be plenty of room under those urban rocks. . . . But the clothes, the rules! A world of them. I didn't think I could do it.

Finally, it was back up my trudge, the stairs. I'd sleep in the cold with my clothes on, windows open, rattle the bars that made up the headboard.

I wanted to do Lennon's primal scream, make first contact.

5

There are no shortcuts in our largely fictional lives. As O'Connor said, "You can do anything you can get away with, but nobody has ever gotten away with much." We have to revise, expunge, because that's the only way our stories find their form, meaning.

No sin can get the final say.

Jesus lives here—in a little village with heated up, twisted plastic soldiers.

(You needed a red hot pin to create grizzle. On your childhood dresser.)

I had a father in World War II.

Guadalcanal.

At this point in my young youth, as Muriel Spark put it, I decided that I probably should go to gradual school. There was nowhere else physically to go to. I could hitch to California, but why? The Mommas and Pappas had split up. And the exterior tiles on my tower at the Prince had begun to lose their luster and sparkle, their fairytale allure. (You could hear them hit the ground outside.)

I got tired of looking out my window mid-mornings—waiting for absolutely nothing to happen, smoking joint after joint, hash; desultory practice on a beat-up guitar. (It *is* a percussion instrument.) I'd put away my beat lyrics, walk downtown, walk back again.

Like any good foster mother, college would have to take me in.

It was odd. As much as I loathed those ivory towers, as much as I still do, I've always found myself coming back. (I would end up teaching at one for decades.) You just have to keep putting quarters into the little college TV sets, work the five channels, the VHF and UHF. Nothing much would actually come through the thing; bits and pieces maybe, old Stroh's commercials. "Read a can of beer tonight."

In any case, if you didn't know where you were going, if you didn't know what fake to shake, you could latch onto the breast of your mother, swing like Remus at the Savoy until things became clear.

Our dearest Alma Maters.

Grad classes were offered at night, a perfect fit.

I signed up for two cross-listed puppies: Modern Poetry and Creative Writing. Some Hunter College lady for the latter, a Dr. Turn; she appreciated economy, wit, syntax gnarled and shunted until it tapped (you) out. And even if her syntactical leaps sometimes escaped me, I liked her pose, admired her judgment, wry repose.

She didn't like my blue-collar work, found it sloppy, over-stated, lacking in, how did she put it, sustained line intensity, focus. She was right of course. I could be rude, over-bearing, clever even. But I didn't have a whole piece of anything. It was kind of like my life.

Performance art!

I looked at my poems as Beat jazz symphonies, offered to the unrepentant. (I needed to read on my knees, circling our seminar table.) The mash I insisted, was deliberate; it was all urban self-destruct, clown work, for both my and my audi-ence's sake, whatever our poses.

(My sense of original sin—if you squinted!)

I needed to urinate on a poem while writing it.

It was the least I could do.

I met a couple of crass Americans in class (the only kind). George, the star pupil, was gifted, Jewish—perhaps the result of the chosen business. He thought as much; you could tell that. To his credit, though, he always seemed a step ahead of everyone else academically. He'd whip together publishable poems and first-rate papers at the drop of a hat. Six foot tall, slightly overweight, he strode around in a long black coat, an anarchist for all the world to see, with a perpetual two-day beard.

He wore his race anger like his ability, striding confidently through our sessions, never taking notes, acing everything. His personal loathing actually endeared him to others in some way. Maybe because his rage, hatred, weren't inverted. They were the result of him trying to measure up to the Measureless, him reacting to the unfairness of the whole situation. His loathing, if directed your way, was usually nothing personal at its root. It was an outgrowth of what he was forced to deal with every day.

No easy task for a secular Jew.

My grouse was more personally fashioned, a braid of laurel, woven out of wasted time – from a life that simply would not cohere. It was ornate, baroque, gratuitous; full of self-adulation, loathing. (Not uncommon ground for the wounded.) In my way. I sought a death large and unclean enough, one that would comment on all I saw I wasn't.

A personal triumph, without the bother or proof of real applause.

I met two other long-term friends in my other class as well: Periwinkle and Miroslav. Periwinkle was and is to this day a butterfly if I've ever met one. At least on the most obvious level. Spry as a young woman could be back then, she had a good deal of Tinkerbell in her step, a fine, illumined intelligence – with more depth than I could see. She delighted in pun, word play, was prone to skipping down halls in bib overalls, to climbing monkey-bars at all hours.

She reveled in wit, still laughs more cleanly at her own jokes than anyone I've ever met. Language for her was some high half-vapor, half-crystal edifice she could sport around in, a place where she could place her joy, subvert her mother. She was blonde, attractive in an ethnic Eastern European sort of way: high cheekbones, deep brown eyes, with graceful nose, one which slopes nicely after an initial rise, a modest chin. (She had a way of turning her head back then, like the short-haired blond Muppet rock star lady. Janice!)

Like George, she was gifted. She made great ceramic pots as well as poems: bright day-glow orange, unusually tall, sealed containers with lions' heads, queen bees with crowns, red doily-imprinted flowers, blue zippers down their green glazed stems.

The other student, Miroslav, was an older guy, about twenty-six or so, with a slightly bulbous nose, blue eyes, thinning hair. He liked to laugh and drink, had a sense of humor that relied on quip, self-deprecation. There was something very likable about him. Maybe it was the fact that he didn't appear to take himself seriously, or the fact that underneath it all he really did, too seriously, and that we all knew, felt on some level, that he didn't like what he saw.

Both he and Periwinkle asked me to join the literary magazine staff after a few post-class skull sessions. (She was the editor-in-chief.) Turned out they had asked George, too. The office was downstairs in the student building, in the same artificially partitioned room with the (gay) film society and the Black newspaper.

(Abdul Khabir, a fine poet! The line I remember: "Sardine cans stacked higher than the misery they hide.")

Each group tended to find its own hours, so there wasn't much interaction.

Periwinkle opened two drawers stuffed with submissions and said "Help" meekly, then re-grouped. "Give me your tired, your weary, your clichéd," she dramatized, swinging up one arm, the other pressing the letters to her breast.

"I say we get a fifth of Cuervo some Saturday afternoon and plow through this stuff. By after six or seven it should all begin to come into focus," Miroslav suggested.

By this time, though, George was already into a stack, quickly dismissing the first two submissions. "Hey, you don't have to read every poem, you know."

He grabbed a large fistful and suggested we go down the hall to the student bar for some za and beer.

We soaked in the suds, fifty cent slices of pepperoni at the pub, trading jibes at the poor unfortunate whose submission we just happened to have in hand at that time.

They were all pretty bad, but who deserved this?

"Writers," George answered.

After far too much beer, a stint of table dancing, Miroslav took his leave. And George, responding to the lull that followed, suggested the three of us go over to his place for medicinal purposes.

I noticed the button on his coat as we walked out to his car: "Drugs are for sick people."

He liked the irony (but missed the advertisement).

His car was a classic, a bomb, an old Camaro with a bad heater, a glass-packed muffler, some flames painted long ago on the rusted sides. In his good-sized, old apartment building, not far from the Potter's Shelf, he played the Persuasions and talked, a controlled smoke funneling in front of him, about his mother. She'd push God Himself into law school if she could.

"Too late," I said. He liked that, passed the thin jay.

Above the mantle in his living room was his shrine, he said, to Our Lady of Bruce Springsteen. Plastic flowers filled a vase underneath the poster-sized framed picture, next to small incense holders. And albums! Crates of them. I was amazed, asked for "Inna Gadda da Vida," but he said he only had one copy.

He uncloaked his felt dust collector for each record, ran it carefully over the vinyl, never touching the grooved part with his fingers. He handled each as if it were a holy relic, palms along the sacred edges, seemed to like older music as he played us Patti Smith's *Horses*, some Little Feat, Randy Newman. Concerned with modulation, he tried to create the ideal atmosphere to get buzzed in. Wry, hip. The Band in real life, just a little down home, a nice intellectual cabin by the creek. A place where nobody would get bored for the time they were there.

It was a generous gesture, maybe a little self-serving.

(Big boat there.)

Periwinkle had her own karma, bounced around the room for a while, arranging pictures, then left, disappeared into the kitchen as he fired up another jay.

"The Ohio Valley. Isn't that the most polluted area in the country, home of Jimmy the Greek, Dean Martin, Traci Lord?"

I had to smile.

"We decided to move to Fargo, but came up short.... Hello, Cleveland." I exhaled.

"Fargo, what the hell is in Fargo? You wanted to get to know some beef cattle more personally?" He sucked hard on his thin weapon. "Sounds like fiction to me."

"No, I stick to poetry. Bukowski among the ruins."

"He sucks. A literary-wanna-be in wino's disguise. For every lazy no talent asshole who dreams of being truly decadent. Somebody ought to shoot that fucker." He went into the kitchen, brought back two Grolsch's, handed me one.

"So, be honest. You don't like him, do you?"

"Give me Roth, Malamud, Delmore Schwartz. Real writers. The unachievable. Assholes who took the time." He took a long drink.

"The Jewish camp?"

I should've helped it—but he seemed obsessed.

Some tension followed.

"Well, I can't argue," I finally said, tossing a pillow I was holding up into the air, catching it again, trying to regain ground. "Those guys are good.... I like your poems, by the way."

We eventually found ground, got good and toasted before long. I told him I planned on burning the next poem I brought in while I was reading it. He said I was a weird guy, but shook his head approvingly. Apparently, he could relate.

(I could "laugh and cry in a single sound.")

It was about this time I got onto Jeffers, *Tendril and the Mesh*. Rexroth's translations from the Chinese, Japanese, Pound there. *The North American Book of the Dead*.

I liked the rough darkness in the first two, the oriental restraint. A novel concept. Levy was his own can of worms.

Every Beat poet in Cleveland has to spend some time with him.

I tried to, literally.

I'd walk with the ghost of Darryl Alfred up Old River Road, reading "Suburban Monastery Death Poem" as I went. Maybe I could do my bit, eventually join him in covering the city with lines, crosshatch his.

I still felt like I was too young in the (pen) nub to participate, but I did go to one of the first junkyard readings. I had to hear more people doing it.

Lots of egos, some good lines, it seemed to me.

You could catch lots of interesting people around town back then: Christopher Franke, Russell Atkins, Daniel Thompson, Barbara Angell, James Kilgore.

I worked in my little garret, managed to publish a few forgettable poems.

On one of those boring sunny winter Saturday mornings, a new blanket of melting snow over the parking lot, the birds were out and singing, fresh little droplets of cold water, running slowly, clearly, down the still frigid supporting telephone wires.

Absolutely nothing was happening (again), so I decided I would go downtown, take the first interesting-looking bus I could find, and fare forward, see what a new day might offer. The one I chose, a 21, was not a Voyager – that would come later. This bus was an RTA job that took me through of slice of middle America to suburban Parmatown, a good-sized mall for all citizens.

It was big and busty, glitz and neon: Amurica, home of
the eternal florescent buzz. Everything was here under tubes
of light. Everything to keep you from thinking. Stuff to wear,
stuff to eat, stuff to keep you off your seat; all of it well past
what was necessary, for anybody. Better trousers, the latest
cut of whatever slice of the better life you could be talked into
consuming, to fill up what was lacking in your own.

A huge cynical laugh, it seemed to me. (I engaged in my
own.) Rich white men, watching the masses reinforce their
twisted dollar-sign perspectives. Pavlov's dogs, coming and
going. It seemed to be a matter of "where there's nothing you
get what you can."

I joined in because I had nothing else going on, hit the food
court for chili dogs. The clang and ring of the pinball arcade
looked like it could offer distraction from distraction, but I
was rescued by Periwinkle, the young woman herself. I saw
her walking out in the mall with her babushka-ed, limping
cane of a mother.

Fun.

"What's happening?" I said to my friend, then turned to her
mom. "And this must be your nice mother, about whom I've
heard so much! . . . And how are you today, ma'am?"

I walked with the family group as they shopped, made my
provocative comments whenever possible. (What else were
friends for?) The older woman kept bullying and buying for
the younger, talking success every step of the way.

"But Mrs. Fetkowski," I asked, "success is such a relative
thing, don't you think? I mean what does that even mean?"

"To you, maybe, but we know what it is," she said, rallying
her body from rack to rack, looking at nice silk blouses. She
had a pair of those thick nylons on, rolled to her knees. "Doc-
tors, lawyers, anchor people. That's success. What good is
intelligence if you don't use it? . . . Things are opening up for
women these days, you know."

"I'm with you in principle," I said. "But anchor people. The

vacuum of space, no? They talk, but how many miles do you
have to travel to get to the next thought? That's the question. . . .
I mean we are talking Dan Rather. . . . I know Periwinkle and
I have talked about this many times over the years, and it's
substance that really matters, don't you think?"

"She can do both."

"Yes, yes. But think of the professional pressure. Be shallow or
die. . . . As the Good Book says, if I can wake up every morning
and look at the stubbled face in the mirror without shame, I
mean, what more could a young and relatively handsome and
available man ask for?" I said to her, batting my eyelashes.

"I like this one," she said. "Such a talker, now you should
be lawyer."

"Or an anchor."

She playfully hit me with her cane.

Periwinkle tried to move the conversation elsewhere, but I
was having too much fun.

"Periwinkle has so many talents, maybe she should think of
sharing them with others. Perhaps something in the service
fields?"

"Tried it. Ran away."

"Well, then, maybe a more inner thing. I know. Something
where she could herself be the challenge? Maybe the arts:
ballet, graphology?"

"Just stop it, will you guys?" Periwinkle said, cutting in.
"This is my life, you know!"

"Okay," I said. "Geez, I'm just trying to help. . . . I'm hurt,
now."

Her mother laughed.

"Miss Sensitive," her mother sniffed. "Here, try these on."

They invited me over, lived in a little suburban box house,
with all the other ticky-tockies on their street.

It made me cringe a little—success, near the bottom of the
suburban ladder! (They'd never take me alive. "Take the skin-
heads bowling." I wanted to play Woody Allen in a corner, my

hands over my ears, me making loud noises. La la la.)

The mother turned to her daughter. "Are you coming to church later, or are you still reassessing? . . . How about you?" she asked me.

"Me?" I said, taking off my shoes, after their fashion. "I'm Anglican Unitarian Bilocationist . . . strictly Bible. We're hoping the papists will come around."

"A sense of humor, Bubka. You could do something with this one."

Periwinkle was already halfway down the basement stairs, in a hurry to get some space.

We had a good time, hopping around, playing an old game of Twister. She got slightly embarrassed when I fell on her, the first time almost accidentally. I tried to play their old ukulele. Her father was a policeman, a captain, and there were framed photos, promotion citations hung all around, a collection of little plastic cops from many lands, each one with a bobbing head.

After I did a little coaxing, I got her to sit down and play some Mozart on their piano: tendons, tight ropes in the backs of her hands. Groaning at her every error (there weren't many as far as I could tell), she played nicely, stuck with it until she finished, then closed the lid, anxious to move on to something else.

"Thank you, boyz," she said bowing in her best Lawrence Welk. "I'm really much better on the violin," she said, pulling one sleeve down to her wrist. "I played in a small orchestra for a while. Not a very good one, but it was fun."

Talk got around to future things. She recounted her various majors: Music, Art, Anthropology, Secondary Ed., Physical Therapy, English, and now maybe Physics. She had started college at sixteen, and now, four years later, was still only a second quarter junior.

I could relate.

(The answers never work. Besides, I hated success. I didn't want much, but not that.)

A woman in my life would have certainly helped me, but how could I saddle anyone with what I was?

Her family's modest possessions all around me – they didn't help. You had to fight to keep all of this stuff! And why? I didn't want to vacate my life to find some temporary mid-suburban fix. There had to be a better reason.

I couldn't figure out how or why she did it, live there with her mom and dad, the outdated kitsch.

I finally made excuse, gave her a friendly hug, smiled, and took my peaceful walk down her driveway.

My room was still empty (smaller) when I got back, dirt crowding in from the corners of the linoleum floor, some so worn that the black tacking underneath came up through the gray base, red and gay sporadic bar designs on top of that. I listened to some jazz, tried to nap. I read some Baudelaire out loud, almost white in the moonlight. The broken glass outside my hermitage sparkled on the sidewalk.

I stood in the window – like a painting.

The whole thing, life, made no sense to me, seemed to promise exactly nothing.

I had never, in my whole life, now that I thought about it, met a person whom I finally admired. The more you got to know someone, the more clear their peculiar nexus of psychoses became – until you just had to walk away, get as far away from them as possible.

Life was like the Bataan Death March, only you got to be the guards, too.

I went to a disco bar on 30th and Euclid, drank, blacked out.

I woke up there the next morning on a strange couch in Fremont, Ohio, with no idea how I had gotten there. A large woman named Betty was very kind (which put me off my stride), offered me some breakfast, nice cheesy eggs; but pieces of my head kept falling into my hands. Then some guy named Bob showed up to join our party; he offered me a glass of orange juice.

He was studying for the ministry, seemed nervous and neat. He thanked me for the theological discussion we'd had the night before.

How drunk was I?

I talked until it felt like I'd answered their charity, then split in the cold. I had to get back.

6

What was the deal with this God show, Gideon's?

Where was Sister Mary Allen (or my third grade teacher) now that I needed them?

No homework—nose in a blackboard circle; lean in, slacker. Like that would help.

Other people would show up, though—a good. That's how life happens for everyone.

Changes always come to us through the folks we meet. Friends, acquaintances, strangers are the ones most responsible for how we grow (or don't). They are our mirrors, mentors, our stumbling blocks.

They're the poems that make life happen.

I had previously made arrangements to see Judy that night, so, as I hitched back in the chilly air, I felt my hopes begin to rise.

She greeted me at the door, the same old Judy, styled up a bit perhaps, fluffed hair, but her lipsticked smile was warm. The new place seemed to house more plants, cats, and parakeets than I remembered. And a new friend!

"Hi, my name's Gauge," the shortish, suited professional woman said, rising up from the couch, extending her hand. We sat and talked a bit as Judy left to rummage through another room.

Gauge was a lawyer, someone who loved new spiritualities, sweat lodges.

She seemed to function as a kind of life coach.

When Judy returned to the room, she carried four medium sized rocks in her arms. "So much is changing for me, James. I've been breaking new ground, opening up. Come on out back. I want to show you something. . . . This gets to it."

I bundled back up, and the three of us went out in the snow, next to their garage, where a circular bunch of stones had been planted in the earth – in every possible compass point except for the four most obvious. At this point, Gauge blessed the four larger stones and supervised her friend, as Judy carefully planted each one.

She smiled. "I like to get into the spirit of this place, of our Native America."

Then she took my hand and patted it, led me over to an outdoor bench in the dark. She reached beneath it and pulled out two small rolled mats.

We proceeded to kneel at each of the four points where she offered up a humming sound, then what appeared to be spontaneous puffs of prayer. Gauge focused our attention, doing a kind of voice-over: "We pray to the West for the wind which brings forth the wide seasons and all change. We pray for pure spring rain, successive veils of healing, quilting the living earth, for our brother trees and plains who have been wounded by the snows of greed, consumerism, for our brothers and sisters the animals: the humpback whales, the baby seals, the spotted owls, the creepers, honey creepers, shearwater, for the fish: the darters, the madtom; for the grizzly bears; for all those creatures which live in and by the good. We pray that you heal those who would destroy our natural dwelling place, the forests, to build more useless square housing.

"We pray to the South, the giver of life and moisture, to the fertile snake and green goddess, that he might penetrate our consciousnesses tonight with wisdom. We pray that our actions might reflect the good that is nature, what we find in the coming of greening leaf and in the motion of the caterpillar on its twig; we pray for every kind of fertility, for the opened bare hands of our woods; may we live in her and find her friend.

"We pray for the East, to the origin spirit; may she breathe life like sunshine into all creatures, may her breath, the breath of each new day, take us, inspire us into becoming our better selves. May we rise up with her each dawn and help her give new outlines, definitions to objects, to the days, the world around us. May each new day sweep across the fields, the rivers, and into the cities and the hearts of people everywhere. May we breathe in our new beginnings. May that never end.

Judy took the last leg.

"And finally, we pray to the cold one, the hard one, the North, the breaker of backs and branches; to our elder brother, Death, the end and taker of all things; and to snow, the season we are in. May we greet him like our own deaths, like the old friend he is, the friend who walks beside us every day, when our time comes, when our cup is full. He gives life even as he daily takes. He is the mouth we speak with. Help us to grow like the good and life-giving fungus out of and into every passing thing. Help us to raise our voices among the trees, the happy remaining leaves!"

More *Tibetan Book of the Dead* stuff?

Couldn't say.

We sat on the chilly bench, smoked some weed. "Sounds like you've got it sorted," I said, "poetically!"

"It's only the goddess within. A movement against greed, insanity, the myth of the machine."

"Our Lady of Mt. Rushmore, pray for us! . . . Are there mile markers?"

"I suppose there are. . . . I'll let you know when I find them."

We both laughed.

"So how's the plunge going?" she asked.

"Hey, come on. At least I've got direction. Geez."

She pushed me lightly at the shoulder. "Dork. Come on, let's go inside."

From the couch she continued, Gauge in the kitchen. "I need to allow myself a slower pace, the pace of the seasons. To hurry is to rob nature of her ways. It's her world, you know."

"Where's Liz?"

"Oh, with Janet. She prefers women these days. Why do you ask?"

"No reason. But tell me, how am I supposed to keep nature's ways in the middle of a square warehouse?"

"Perhaps it's the wrong work?"

"For everyone?"

"I wouldn't doubt that!"

"Or maybe it's just the real world, sweet though it is."

"But we've got to make this thing work, James. Can't you see? Coyote is our only chance. We've got to re-tell the story, the world; we've got to slow things down, build the first house."

I heard the back door close quietly.

Earth by April's food was wholesome, tasty, if a little heavy on Medusa's hair-sprouts, those small invidious counter-cultural fingers. Everyone there was so relaxed, chilled, that I found myself becoming a bit nettled. It seemed a little self-congratulatory, gnostic.

I told myself to lighten up.

Judy began to talk about her past lives, about Egyptian high culture, what it was like to live along the Nile: fine baths and slaves, a game, not unlike cribbage. She described Apis cult rituals in minute detail, said she's known Edward Bach, was at Queen Mary's court in other lives.

"Bach invented flower remedies. Three drops, four times a day and you can get over just about anything. . . . Open up. I was feeling lonely the other day, took some essence of heather, and, bang, it was gone. There's a whole reality happening here that consumerism, empiricism have stolen from us. . . . If I'm having trouble learning by experience, there's the chestnut bud. The list goes on."

And she did.

She cried out for world hunger, for dog restraints to truck beds; she discoursed on enzyme dieting, on the warming Gaia, on the efficacy of crystals.

There were some nicer, quieter, more congenial moments.

Though they didn't, couldn't last. There was just too much manufactured peace here, and what is poorly made always seems to have a short shelf life.

I wanted what was real: Sister Mary Allen throwing some kid through the lockers in eighth grade because he'd dyed his hair (probably gambled as well).

Tough love, violent love? This suburban stuff seemed fluff, a way to get your own way while appearing altruistic. On the other hand, maybe Judy just needed to release some spores.

I thought of Shirley MacLaine in her fourth life, doing the frug.

Walking her home, I cut the whole thing short, as quietly as I could. I said I needed to think about all of this. This wasn't what I needed. She was nice, I knew that, but she sounded like *Cosmopolitan* magazine, something for the terminally hep. Lots purchased – nothing gained.

There was a good impulse there, so I tried to be kind. And God knows I could certainly be as quick as anyone else to jump off the nearest pointless cliff. But at the same time, I couldn't make this world pretty just by using my (Barney) imagination.

The darker questions, places, seemed more real, pressing. The North.

7

By the following Tuesday, looking in the cracked mirror above my papered fireplace, I could see I was not the fairest in the land anymore. I had Thomas Campion's surreal shopping bags under my hung-over eyes, an unruly brush on my face; I needed a haircut and was beginning to warm to my own smell.

I tried sleeping on the benches downtown at nights, but the cops wouldn't have any of that. I'd have to find new bars, drink alone. Finally, in my want I bought a ticket, took a Greyhound back down to Conurbation. I don't know what I expected to find there. A six-pack under my arm, I walked through the high grass above the steel mills, then along the banks of the Ohio, with its cold brown swirls, the whole place coughing like James Wright (soon) in Italy.

My only living relative was an aunt who lived in Denver.

It was like I'd never lived in southeastern Ohio, or anywhere for that matter, the water closing behind the coal barges, the iron oblivious sumac that would last longer than I.

I rented a room for one night, slept downtown with the mold, the cockroaches.

On the bus back the next day, I thought of God, of quitting my job, of doing the country by bus. All the poor outside – and in: seated women with their gone bawling smudged-faced children-with-a-chance; the dirty-haired soldiers who only had their uniforms to recommend them; the gone, Hunter Thompson's doomed, the auditory hallucinators.

I didn't think I could take that – though I doubted I would have stuck out.

Maybe I could hitch my way around the country, find railroad work as I went. Kerouac or Least Heat Moon on the hotfoot. As evening came on that night back in Cleveland, I wandered around the streets near campus, stopping every now and then under a streetlight to read from Rilke's elegies out loud (to the moon) – those and a Wright poem I'd copied and put, folded up, in those pages: "Autumn in Martin's Ferry, Ohio."

What kind of life was this?

A few of the empty buildings on Euclid added light to the proceedings. One sported an advertisement for a workshop on centering prayer. I went in, more bored than anything, walked down a well-lit hallway where I met a small man with squinting eyes, glasses; longish, slightly unruly hair. He said his name was Lee, he welcomed me. There were a few old couches around back there, a TV set in a common room. Offices, it looked like, to the right. I was going to ask him where I was when he offered coffee or hot chocolate.

"Free lunches. Cool."

I followed him to the industrial-sized percolator, hot water, Styrofoam cups. They were the only things in that room except for the light green paint on the walls. It looked like a place for early union meetings. I asked about the sign.

"Centering prayer?" he answered. "Be here now. The only dance there is . . . and there is only the dance."

"Rum Dum, Eliot. Nice. But the center pre-supposes itself, doesn't it?"

"For you to decide, I suppose," he answered. "Maybe the place where you stop traveling in and begin traveling out?"

"You sound like a fortune cookie."

"Fair enough. But, welcome. Let me say that at least! . . . We're having a coffee-house tonight if you're interested in that sort of thing."

I needed more info, but a student loudly called him from down the back hallway.

I heard some strumming and so moved past them, into the back part of the building. It was a pretty big space, some folkie playing Bob Dylan. The guy sang like he was mouthing the definitive cultural statement, solemn honey dripping from the lips of the next poet in line.

The room was sparely populated, a few light-hearted young women bouncing on a couch in the way back, along the wall farthest from that voice. I walked back, past the vacant candle-lit tables: amber colored glasses, white mesh around them.

I liked the two immediately, their enthusiasm in the face of all this painful music. I listened as unobtrusively as possible, standing there next to the couch, facing the singer.

They were singing the Mickey Mouse Club song in Spanish!

I couldn't resist, I turned to them, hopped up and down in counterpoint said, "Hi, my name's Cubby. . . . What's yours?"

Terry and Joy.

I liked their enthusiasm. Their view of life seemed comic, which in itself seemed so to me. But they were oblivious, both to my shirt sleeve angst and, apparently, to the absurdity of college life in general. College was weird; they got that. But it was okay as far as they were concerned, too, like a lot of life; they seemed to accept things at face value. They went to their classes, apparently, jumped through the required hoops, and then with luck, would find a job.

"And a husband," I asked, "an MRS degree?" Joy became mock dreamy. Terry shrugged, started bouncing again.

Life seemed to be about what they expected, and, as I continued to talk, it became clear that the whole process was no big deal to them. This was planet earth we were talking about, after all. They did what they had to do to get where they wanted to go, tried to find some fun along the way.

"What about injustice?" I demanded. "What about the plight of the ever-present Native American whales, the collective sighing of the rain forests? Listen, you can hear it if you try." Unfortunate, bad, they both agreed as they came to a halt, Terry rubbing her chin. But they regrouped, looked at each other, smiled, then started with the bouncing again, this time singing half the song in English: "Hey there, hi there, ho there, we're as happy as can be.... Mickey Mouse, Pato Donald."

Then they stopped, leaned into each other, laughing.

"Weren't there things past humor?" I wanted to know. One shook her head yes, the other, no; then they started bouncing some again.

"Are you going to Mass?" Terry asked me. "We could pray for the Native Americans there. That would be a start anyway."

I was stunned.

(Lee! Sneaky baistard!)

"Yes, you may join us," the priest said as he moved over to a cabinet, began to vest in denim. "I was going to do my sermon on the world 'schizophrenia.' It means 'broken-hearted.' Might be too much, though. I don't know." He smiled a little at my consternation. "Hey, you don't have to go if you don't want to, you know? Many people don't. Just make yourself at home. Lots of people here aren't Catholic. Take a load off, talk to the natives."

I left, walked the mile or so it took to get to the square downtown. Then I walked back.

Apparently, the earlier singing had only been a prelude, because things were now in full swing. Couples were scattered about, some guy singing a lame song about the prodigal son. It only took me a moment to spot Terry, sitting there by herself with her long blond Polish hair, her graceful nose, profile. She wore her glasses like an older woman's, low on her nose.

"Hey, where's Tweedle-Dum?"

"You mean Ms. Reiner?" she half-laughed. "She had to go study for a bio test. We missed you at Mass." I ignored the comment.

"May I?"

"Sure," she said with less than total enthusiasm. "There's always room for one more around here."

"Or more . . . So what's the story with this God guy, any-way? . . . Do you spook little kids on Halloween with sparklers, day-glow MIDNIGHT COWBOY crucifixes? . . . What about genocide, over-population? Where's He at with that?"

"Whoa . . . slow down. . . . Your name is James, right?" She extended her hand, shook mine. "How are you? . . . Now, what was the question? Halloween?" She scratched her head. "A strange one. . . . Some people don't celebrate it. I don't know. Maybe that's a good idea. Nobody goes around dressing like saints. . . ."

"What about the hunger thing? I'm taking a survey."

"Geez, come up for air, will you? I came over here to forget about philosophy."

I paused.

"Well, you guys seem so up-beat, what's up with that? Are you on something? Can I get some?"

"Well, prayer helps, though I don't want to sound like the answer woman. I'm not."

"But, really, come on. What kind of God allows for world starvation? And why inflict the poor Africans? Why not the Europeans, especially considering what they've been up to for the past six-hundred years?"

She sighed.

"The way I look at it is that sin is an expression of freedom. But it never gets the final say. Nobody gets past personal respon-sibility – because other people matter."

"I don't know anybody who's free. Oh, they talk that stuff, but then it's one pellet or another, isn't it? . . . Whenever one of you religious types can't explain something, you take the one called 'mystery.'"

"Well, what isn't? . . . Sometimes I look up at the night sky. All that order. How could there be an end to that? . . . But if something comes after, that just prolongs the question. And yet, how could something not end? Everything I know has an ending."

"Except this example."

"Come on now. Play fair."

"Is there a stone so large God can't lift it?"

"I don't know any of that. When it comes down to it, for me, I find what I need in the love of Jesus Christ, the God-Man. He died for me. What else matters in the end?"

"Did he invent hell? . . . A cold idea, to quote Dante."

"Dante, geez," she said, looking over her glasses. "That's by me. . . . We choose hell all the time, don't we? The ugly comment, thought, small thefts. . . . The saints say that God suffers every slight, for every soul. That's Calvary."

"To the rescue."

She made a face, so I pulled back.

I looked away, then looked at her again. She was a beauty all right. That hair, those dimples, her pale skin, cheekbones. She obviously enjoyed merriment, in gesture, in her slightly hyperbolic reactions. She knew she was attractive; how could she not? But she didn't seem too vain about it. Occasionally, when she was thinking, she'd ride her long blond hair up the back of her swan neck.

God was real because He was so to her.

No way in there.

Middle class, but I had to admit that her life beat mine. She valued things, had a sense of direction.

"Would you like my phone number?"

She gave me a quizzical look. . . . "Maybe you should go on a retreat. That might help you to slow down. . . . There's this Catholic farm up in Canada I think about going up to once in a while. . . . I've heard it's a bit conservative. Still, it sounds nice. I like the idea of shucking corn. . ."

"What's up, man problems?"

"Is the Pope Catholic?" she asked. But that was as far as she wanted to take that.

She wrote down their number on a piece of paper, slid it over to me.

"Give me yours, too, just in case."

"Okay," she relented. "But don't call me for any dates."

"He must be a tough nut."

"Go, go, leave. I want to listen to some more of this good music."

I looked at her number, the phone number for the farm.

I left the window open in my room that night. It was cold on the bed, as was fitting, breath-cold, shoes-on cold.

I felt like I existed outside of life. I was always looking for what I couldn't find.

But I didn't want to die in a dump like that.

I needed some kind of life first, have a go at one anyway.

And so, though I couldn't see strong hands reaching up from the dark, icy water for me yet, I could feel the frigid caverns — the movement the ripples were beginning to make. If there was something, anything to find, I wanted, no, I needed to find it.

Barry was right.

No one gets out of here alive. But the Prince Albert-in-a-can wasn't where I wanted to be found, with a bad poem crumpled in my hand.

I needed. I needed something more. That was always it.

So I called Canada — the Pristine — tried to sound as Catholic as I could. It might not be the answer, but it would be some-where else, maybe closer to it.

Surprisingly, they were receptive.

We set a date.

If I didn't like it, I figured, I could hitch my way around the Great North or rent a cabin in northern Idaho — buy a used Harley, get me one of those "Then Came Bronson" hats.

I could try his taciturn thing.

(I couldn't imagine anyone complaining much about that.)

I took in some Catholic services around town, their Mass, bided my time. It was a different world, one I'd forgotten, with statues, vaulted ceilings, and altars; little Oz red lights, enough vested priests and deacons to change the world.

There was an odd sort of beauty there, a loneliness.

Those two things seemed to belong together. I liked that, but couldn't figure out the dynamic.

And what the heck was up with the flat bread? The Eucharist: that's what they called it. (Some memories remained.)

I felt some tension at the prospect of having to deal with quiet rural types on a regular basis. On the other hand, their world did offer some order; a weird one, but beggars couldn't be choosers. They seemed welcomed.

("Here comes everybody.")

What the heck? I figured. If I were going to go down in the icy water, I might as well sample the available wares. I had to push on, couldn't stop.

You Don't Live Here Either

Across the cages of the keyless aviaries,
The lines and wires, the gallows of the broken kites,
Crucify, against the fearful light,
The ragged dresses of the little children.
Soon, in the sterile jungles of the
    waterpipes and ladders,
The bleeding sun, a bird of prey, will terrify the poor,
These will forget the unbelievable moon.

> "Aubade – Harlem," Thomas Merton
> – for Baroness C. de Hueck

1

I wonder if Bob Dylan knew what kind of confetti party favor he was showering his public with when he released *Slow Train Coming* and *Saved*, in '79 & '80. More than likely, he didn't care. After all, he'd been through all that before. The left was still reeling from the Tom Paine Awards in 1963. The first singing Beat had made it quite clear then that he would be no one's running dog, no matter the virtue (real or apparent) involved.

See Newport, Forrest Lawn.

But this time around many of the pious right got on board as well. They felt betrayed, too, especially those who found his new Christian fast-food "I am the unerring prophet" theology creakily fundamental.

I was one of those. I'd spent two years in Adoration, praying for him and Woody Allen after all! (One out of two isn't bad.) He was supposed to become a Catholic.

Both sides were too full of themselves to move.

They still are.

Whenever we try to save others from some version of hell, we end up creating our own.

What right do we ever have to object to anything?

It was his road, his heart. And it wouldn't have mattered if he were doing the Vineyard Christian Fellowship or a Hari Krishna county-jail orange sari thing (who didn't love those little finger cymbals!), or if he suddenly gave himself over to re-doing Rimbaud or Verlaine, dressing in drag.

God chooses, but He also allows a longer path for everyone, each one of them different, each one part of a necessary process.

Our job is to love and to stay out of His way. (Have my sins been less egregious? We only see acts, after all, never the mitigating personal history, never the heart.)

T. S. Eliot probably had to deal with the same thing in 1927 when Leonard Woolf insisted that his new conversion was simply a way for him to try and become more English. We can work to make the impulse to adjudicate sound as wry, fashionable, and underhandedly self-affirming as possible. But the package is small, however it comes.

Within a week I was on a muzzled Greyhound heading into the Great White North—destination: Combermere, Ontario. I'd waved goodbye to my All-American college life. George and Periwinkle having wished me happy trails; she congratulated me for choosing real life over academic blather; George told me to fare forward, Voyager, recommended low to no—profile, that is, that I keep my sails out of the water. Anyone prone to such absurd careening might be worth reading someday.

Clueless, on a bus, my duffel bag stowed underneath, I played out my options. I wondered how I was going to convince these people that I was in earnest about their religion without sounding like the complete phony I was. Maybe some choked reticence? A kind of tacit, respectably distant fawn? The Gollum slither?

I didn't have any trouble at the border, told the guy I was going on a retreat.

"Have a nice day, eh," I said with a smile.

"Take off," he smiled back, waving me on my pleasant way.

Toronto was cleaner than I thought possible for a big city. The guard rails on the sides of the Interprovincial coming in were not dented, banged up; there was no flying debris, no dust working the support posts, no overgrown weeds along the sides of the highways. What made these boys tick, I wondered?

I had never been to Britain, so I couldn't really see how much of an effect that had. "Keep Britain tidy," I guess that worked here as well.

And what exactly was a commonwealth? A loose confederacy of nations. Share a queen. Struck me as geeky. And what exactly did they expect to get from old marble-bottom anyway? Wisdom? Certainly not her cash. Canada, O Canada, what bugs were up thy shorts? I'd have to sit back in this alien nation; that much was clear. Let the robot do the talking.

Everyone was so darned pleasant. (It was like we were in Iowa or something.) The bus drivers looked like nicer versions of Chicago policemen, with little Blue Line Voyager hats. (Mayor Dailey would have rolled over on his graves.) I wouldn't have wished America on anyone, but this place gave me the heebie-jeebies.

Too neat.

The bus station in Toronto turned out to be a two-story layer cake, more like a travel agency than a bus terminal. Sculpted concrete, nice, if few, seats inside. No loiterers in Canada, I guessed. Everyone had direction or were encouraged to have some. How did this even belong to the same genus/species as the Greyhound station in Cleveland or the Port Authority in New York, where every scab-infected unfortunate on the earth pitched a tent in front of the TVs, hit you up for a buck, giving you tb in the process?

It didn't look like diseases were allowed in Canada.

But how had they managed that? Socialized medicine? Cold northern virtue? Maybe the whole country wore a powdered wig, a Puritan collar. It was their respectability, denial.

Keep your sins at home. We just don't do that here.

(These days, Canada — and Gary Trudeau — seem a lot like Ireland. Both of them want to be part of Europe so badly that it actually causes them physical pain.)

I boarded a second bus and began to travel northeast. By the time I got to Peterborough, I was ready to jump ship.

Just what the heck was I doing here?

What were the basic tenants of the faith? Wasn't one sup-posed to do something when going into a church? Bless or sprinkle myself, take a quick slug of holy water? (As a kid, I had altar boy friends who used to steal collection basket money.) What was the deal with Mary? The place was named after her. Wasn't she God's funnel? I couldn't remember. Why hadn't I paid more attention? What if I gave myself away, made some wry or accurate comment?

My anxiety waned, though, as I did a quick hike around Peterborough. What were these nice, clean Canadian Catholics going to do to me anyway, throw me to the Canadian lions fer breakfast? Bert Lahrs. The town was clean as a spitless whistle. All the funny money, the slightly taciturn, if smiling folk. I wondered what the insane asylums looked like up here. No need for strait-jackets. Just tell the inmates to sit here, go there. Or if they did have them on, you could watch them skinny along the ground, humping like cartoon worms, cocoons, obeying your every command. I wondered if they had a test to tell who the insane ones were? Or did they just march up, confess it meekly: "I need to be inside, you know. It's true. I have a paper right here. . . . I signed it. . . . It's in orange."

Crayon, big tears.

After a quick look through a liquor store, more like a super-market with rollers than the institutional look you get in the States, I bought a bigger bag of M&Ms, headed back to the bus. I felt so chipper that I even talked to some old lady while we rolled up the perfect highway, ever northward, toward my heavenly death, as Judy would have put it.

It got old, the ride.

Combermere was a long-assed way up there.

I wondered if they had running water, any summer to speak of. I'd find out soon enough, and as late afternoon waned, chilled, I curled some in my seat. In snatches, I watched what looked like virgin forest pass by: more and more birch, pine, fir.

Way too neat.

We stopped for dinner at a restaurant. Kind of a cleaned-up Nebraska, with corn-fed proprietors, friendly, gabby in a local sort of way. The woman behind the register and the driver were old buds, everyone with that often higher-pitched Canadian way of speaking. There was an awful rightness to this place as well, nicely creased napkins and spotless water glasses because it was a place to eat. A fresh bulletin board with notices about the Moose Lodge meetings and Boy Scout jamborees.

("Take the skin heads bowling.")

When I finished my cheeseburger, the cheese squarely on top of the meat, placed perfectly below the slightly dry Presbyterian bun, I stepped outside, finally noticed that it was the snow which had put a squeeze in their voices. It was piled quite high along the edges of the parking lot. It wasn't terribly cold, but I had miscalculated. Spring up here was not running on the same schedule as in Ohio. I would need a winter coat. No stores between here and Combermere either, I bet. Judy's death indeed.

2

I was the only one to get out at my stop, two hours later. It had gotten much colder. The driver followed me down, flipped up the underneath compartment door; I picked out my duffel bag without a word. That was it. Just the exhaust, the middle of a new world. Me and the moose.

I called out in their language. No answer.

Looking at the size of the town, rubbing up my jacket sleeves, my hands, I was surprised it was on the map at all. On my side of the street there was a red barn-shaped general store immediately behind me, no sidewalks, just sand. Its competition: a Western front food store, two doors down on the same side, the indented post office/restaurant in between, a small parking lot in front of them. The only other building on my side was a rent-all place some 400 yards, er, meters, down the road. On the other side of the street, a laundromat, and a very small motel, closed for the season. There was a docking ramp out back of that for what I was to learn was the Madawaska River. Apparently, tourists liked this place in the summer.

The river behind was beautiful: wide, some of it frozen, surrounded by miles and miles of dense forest, the sprinkled salt of birch trees, a collective mild confusion in the branches. That was it, though, as far as the city proper was concerned. I stood out there for a while in the dark, getting cold, wondering just what my next move should be. It was never made clear to me over the phone just where exactly the farm was in relation to the highway, or where I was to be picked up for that matter. I hadn't asked, so I had no choice right then but to stand there, befuddled in my jacket, banks of snow shoveled, eye level on either side of the restaurants.

Finally, I just sat down on my cold duffel bag, in front of my repeating breath, tried to read DiPrima's *Earthsong* in the dim light out front of the general store. After a time, I decided. I'd just have to go across the street, find the house behind that motel and knock. I didn't even have time to reach down and pick up my bag, though, because a van pulled around in front of me, up to the post office door. Some guy got out and deposited a slew of mail into the all-night slot before spotting me. I figured he must be the guy, given the volume, and walked over. "Are you looking for Madonna House?" he asked. "Geez, nobody told me anybody was coming."

Given the obvious organization, I figured I was in for a treat. Maybe a bunch of old hippies ran the place.

That might be nice. (Hopefully, some loose women might be involved.)

"Ah have," I said, going for early Southern humor, but it was like he didn't even hear me.

"And, jeepers, no winter coat. Come prepared, eh? You could've frozen out here. . . . Hop in." He had a fine Irish brogue, youngish fellow, about thirty or so, with a long red beard.

"Got any cough drops?"

"You like it, eh?" he asked, laughing the laugh of leprechauns, pulling down on his Smith Brothers whiskers. "It's a gift from me old grandmother . . ." Then he shifted his tone. "I wonder why no one told me someone was coming."

"God will take care of me." (I had to get the feel of this.)

"Indeed, but a fine winter coat wouldn't hurt now either, would it? . . . Well, best be getting back." The van was bare bones, a second seat behind ours, hinged benches along the back panels which served as flip-top containers. He turned to me. "Welcome to Madonna House. . . . My name is Patrick, and I will be your flight attendant. . . . How did you hear about us, anyway?" I told him about the Newman Center, said I needed to find a good line to walk.

"We can lend you a coat tonight. Tomorrow's a half-day. You can go up to St. Joe's in the afternoon. You'll be able to pick up something cheaply."

"Great."

Nothing much else was said. He only broke the silence to get my name and to point out St. Joseph's Rural Outreach Center which we passed on our way in. As we pulled into the gravel parking lot, I got my first glimpse of the main house. It was an old, well-kept, steep-roofed white building off to the right side of the lot. And judging by how well lit the first floor was, it looked like things were still hopping.

He told me I was too late for dinner, late tea, but that if I were hungry, he could send some bread and jam up to the dorms with the van later. I thanked him, said I was fine, followed him into a door that led down to the building's basement.

The first things I ran into once inside a second door at the bottom of the inside steps were mail slots, stuffed coat racks, rows of neat boots lined up and tucked wherever possible.

"Take off your jacket and boots. I'll introduce you to Dave. He's the RA up at St. Ann's, Joachim's." Feeling like a false lamb, I half slunk after him past curtained bookshelves, a ping-pong table (boxes stuffed neatly underneath), past an upright piano, an old TV along the farthest wall. We proceeded up a narrow flight of stairs to a large, crowded dining area. The first thing I noticed besides all the cliques of animated folks at picnic-like tables yukking it up were the thin metal posts that held up the ceiling in this dining/library area. The kind people used to support sagging basements. Odd, but practical. A better sign.

The wooden tables were simple, covered in gray plastic, stapled underneath; there were benches on either side, end chairs. I felt anxious, as I knew I would, but there was something likable about the place: a floor so old and worn that I could feel the rising knots in the wood under my stockinged feet. Books were neatly shelved everywhere, complete with Library of Congress call numbers, each section titled: Catholic Saints, Mariology, Christology.

There was a big picture of Tolstoy on the wall at the other end, a librarian's desk, a small card catalog. (Why not Dostoevsky? I wondered, since he at least believed in miracles.) And to my immediate left from the top of the basement stairs, a wide set of steps which led to what I was to learn was an upstairs chapel. At the base of those stairs, to the left was a display of Ekaterina Fyodorovna Kolyschkine's books.

I'd never heard of her, but that proved absolutely nothing. Some kind of Swedenborgian, Margery Kempe mystic I guessed, judging by the titles of the books: *Poustinia, Kenosis.* Exotic language for the finer points of Catholic mysticism, no doubt. I leaned over, picked up a book trying not to be obvious in avoiding all the new people.

Some were quite lively, sitting in groups, but some sat by themselves, with little shoe boxes in front of them. They looked to be writing letters. Other people carried trays, empty cups, and pitchers out of the room. It was all noisy, controlled. Having just gone to college, I wasn't used to seeing this many alert people in one place, so I didn't know quite what to make of it.

But before I could continue my evasion, actually read some of the material, Patrick came over and introduced me to Ed, the man who ran the work crew. He was a good-sized guy, my height, but broader, with short hair, lots of energy. He shook my hand, looked right into my eyes, and playfully slapped me on the back. He said I looked like a man who could use the rigors of farm life.

"Not to worry, James. We'll put some gas in that tank."

That stopped me in my tracks.

Where did that come from? What did this guy know about my tank anyway? I might have found a way to flip him off, had it not been for the fact that everyone around me, as if on some unspoken comment, rose.

("They've realized," I said to myself.)

It was 10 o'clock, I was to learn. Time to sing the "Salve Mater." They all knew it by heart, and once again I was thrown in and left to swim. Should I know this? Was it required

Catholic ritual? Finally, I just closed my eyes, wondered how I might be able to make an escape.

There was a bustle of activity after the song. Dave, my RA, introduced himself, had a coat, hat, and gloves for me to try on as he led me through a real maze of people, through the basement. Outside, dressed, duffel bag and jacket under arm, he pointed me to the brown van. Other young men headed in the same direction.

Once inside, all of us shivered in the bitter cold (facing the road in the lot), some jumping up and down in their seats, male guests waiting for Dave who had a few quick errands to run. My pea coat fit me nicely, as did the blue knit hat, a tuque as they called them. I pulled it down past my, by now, freezing ears.

There seemed to be what looked like an enfeebled orchard behind us in the middle of the compound. It was surrounded by an old split-rail fence. A sign post off to our left, like the kind you'd see in a M*A*S*H episode, shook slightly in the wind. So many miles to get to places like Gravelbourg, Saskatchewan, to Carriacou, West Indies, to Flagstone, Arizona, to Freetown, Liberia, to Paris. These were, I was to learn, directions to get to some of their soup kitchens and prayer houses.

Behind the skinny orchard at our backs, I noticed another white house, what looked like a bridge to its right, and some ancient gas pumps between that bridge and the green sheds attached to the main house. On each side of the gravel parking lot I was sitting in there were other houses, both very small, what I was later to find out were the infirmary and an older men's staff house. Women guests walked across the road. I wondered why we had to go to our dorms in a van. Couldn't they find a closer place, especially in this sparsely populated area? Maybe they just wanted to keep us away from the holy babes.

They did.

One guy, shivering next to me, sporting a great square Amish or Orthodox beard, was struggling, trying to roll a cigarette. "Welcome to Ice Station Zero. . . . Colder than a witch's nose. . . . Can you believe this front? . . . Hi, my name's

Mickey." I shook his one hand as he precariously tried to balance his half-rolled cigarette paper in the other. I was a little surprised by his slightly feminine demeanor. But he seemed like a likable fellow. All for one, that kind of thing. "What were we in together *on*?" was my question.

There were ten of us, counting Dave, who eventually piled into the van, all of us in the back laboring to generate heat as the metal beast slowly warmed. We didn't have enough space to genuinely shiver, so a few of the guys made do by jostling into each other, shoulder to shoulder to create some friction, stamping their feet at the same time, beneath the clouds of breath, just to remind their toes who they were a part of. I was introduced to the five guys in my immediately far back vicinity, but the names came too fast, and I forgot them almost immediately.

"They'll be a quiz in the morning," Mickey confided.

I got what I was soon to recognize as the usual volley of questions. Who was I, where was I from, how had I heard of the place? Other splinters of conversation had begun as well, so soon enough my comments were more or less swallowed up as people got back to their own concerns.

I did talk a little bit with a soccer player from New England. Hubert was his name. I told him I was sorry about that. He laughed a little, but seemed strangely silent to me, a taciturn New Hamshirer perhaps. He said he'd come out here to get his life on track. (There was an unwritten rule at Mary's Farm I was to—slowly—learn. Don't ask people about their pasts. But at the time no one had told me about it, so I pried for all I was worth.)

"Why here?" I asked. "Too many drugs, firearms?"

He gave me a pained smile, rubbed his face. "Drugs, yeah. I need a lot of healing. A priest told me about this place. Said it might be a good place to slow down, allow the Lord time to work things out."

"I'm running from the Feds, personally. Boot-legging, prostitution, selling illegal crucifixes." I watched for his response.

Part of him wanted to laugh, but another part of him felt like he was supposed to be put off. "Na," I said. "I'm converting from the Urdu religion. Goat sacrifices. For the snasauges. We worship Washington's eye on the dollar bill."

"Most of us have. . . . I just felt too much pressure out there myself, too many demands. People hounding me about which direction I should take with my life. Here I can put my feet out," and he did so.

"Nice. A joke." We both laughed.

We took a quick left after a couple of miles, and by the time we had finished our eventual turn from the main road, we were there. A smallish white house, a porch. The guy who was in the front passenger seat jumped out immediately, took the key off the ledge just above the door. A silly kind of precaution, really, I thought, considering how far we were away from anyone. Like a person couldn't just break the glass or wouldn't look in that spot first if he were bent on a more mannered version of B&E.

Oh well, roll with the Catholics.

It was only a matter of minutes before we were all in the kitchen. Guys began brushing their teeth in the sink, washing up out of wide white metal bowls, each taking personals: a towel, shampoo, toothbrush from his slot behind a curtained partition, each with the combatant's name taped below it. A few guys in another van came in soon after; they lived down the hill in a more primitive cabin, St. Joachim's, where there were only kerosene lamps and a wood burning stove.

It was very crowded in the small kitchen, noisy. In the next room, the first-floor bedroom, three guys were sitting at a table, discussing whether it was possible to attain perfection in this life. I was too tired from the travel to try and make anything out of the whole scene, wanted just to take a quick shower, get into my hairshirt, and go to bed.

Dave informed me, however, that showers weren't allowed during the week. Well water conservation. He even went so far as to request that I not flush after urination, at least until the bowl was good and yellow. What if we all had low sugar content? I asked, and what about number two?

The outhouse down the hill.

My first venture into the unknown dark night of faith, I figured, as I put my out-to-sea coat back on. The green, upright wooden structure seemed sturdy enough, a little hook on the inside. But it was quite cold by then, and I was worried about sitting on the frigid plastic seat. Would I stick to it? But there it was, on the wall: a Styrofoam doughnut cut-out.

When I finished, I took my time returning, looked up at the stars. Never had I seen them so clearly. The milk in Terry's Way, the gauze in the sky, clear and sharp enough for me to wonder if there were anything to this God business. Was there a place so far away that it had no stars? If there was a God, none of these guys seemed to be getting rich off of Him, at least on the surface of things, that seemed clear enough.

(Was that good or bad?)

Dave directed me upstairs, where I found my bunk among many. They had recently ripped out a partition; I could see the newly sanded and painted strips along the walls and ceiling. Familiar metal posts held the place up. Mickey bunked next to me, to my right, away from the stairs. Jean-Michel from Mon-re-al, came next, then Ted, from Regina, and finally Rich, from the West Indies, by the window. On the other side of the aisle from Rich was a huge, bearded guy, Tom (nicknamed Adam). Nick, from Akron, came next, and then Daoud, a Palestinian Christian Arab.

Daoud commented that we could be an American basketball team because of our height: Ted, Adam, Nick, and myself. Tom, though, seemed slightly put off by that, as he seemed to be by the name he had been given. (He did look like the first man: good-looking fellow, rugged, with prominent, slightly protruding eyebrows.)

I uncharitably thought of Hubert in the van: hospital ward — though I have certainly never been a mental health poster child. (He bunked at Joachim's, down the hill.)

Nick, however, was a different story. Very expansive, he welcomed the world, me included, heartily. He said we could all be monks on Mt. Athos, at least judging by the beards, though he didn't want to discriminate against the clean-shaven.

Daoud called out in a high voice: "May it be so. Christ is risen!"

"Truly," Tom added, perhaps, it seemed to me then, because he had learned to do as much. He certainly didn't seem moved by a noticeable enthusiasm when he said it. Struck me as a little odd. Cult-like behavior?

"We do want to be ready to greet Him when He comes," he added.

"Speak it, brother," said Jean-Michel.

"You and Rich can throw open your windows," said Mickey. "Just in case He comes tonight; stick your feet out to stay alert. Let us know."

Rich smiled, a quiet one.

"I'll think I'll just keep my candle lit," said Nick, crawling cozily under his several covers.

"That's okay by me," said Jean-Michel as he pulled out his double eye-patch sleeping mask, put it on. (Everybody delighted in him wearing this. He also sported red underwear.)

"What are you even doing here? That's what I want to know," joked Tom. Others laughed.

"Taking a vacation. Now if you don't mind, I would like to get some sleep. Call me at eleven, won't you?"

"Yes, your highness," said Mickey. "Crumpets, then, the morning paper?"

"Folded, on the side of the tray."

Someone threw a book in Jean-Michel's general direction. He lifted one wing of his eye-patch.

"Rabble," he sniffed.

Things got quiet quickly, however: a hard day of work it looked like. And then, sometime later, I saw Daoud get up in the semi-darkness before a little icon of Christ that he had placed on his dresser. He prayed there quietly out of a book for a good fifteen minutes, turning the pages, rocking back and forth slightly as he read. Nick saw me watching him from across the room, winked in my direction.

"You just never know about this place," he whispered, smiling. Then he turned over, fell asleep.

I said nothing during the whole course of conversation, wondered how I would get on with these guys, what they would mean to me. As it turned out, most of them just passed through my life like so many others had before them. They each left an impression, favorable mostly, and then they were gone. The story of my life, anybody's, but the story of this place, particularly. People came through all the time. Some would stay for a week, some for a month, some for a year. Those who really liked it found vocation, stayed for what promised to be the rest of their lives. But for most of us, it was a matter of learning to enjoy the place, the people, and then having to leave it all behind: the joy of friendships, the people, the apparent holiness.

3

A bitterly cold morning came earlier than I would have been comfortable with: six a.m. And then the rush again. Dave assigned me a towel and rack, a space, and I washed off as best I could, using leftovers, communal soap. A quick pit job, a floss in Jean-Michel's case. Some shampooed, everyone combed, brushed. Girls at breakfast, had to be. I liked Jean-Michel right off, a French Canadian who mistrusted everyone who wasn't. "Free Quebec," I'd say whenever I passed him. He liked that.

I piled, freezing, into the van with him and Nick, waited for the others. I asked what was next as Nick read: cold, ungloved fingers on his Bible.

"You shall see, my crass American friend. Regimentation. It's all designed to keep us from the girls," smoke puffing in front of the fried Frenchman, both of us stamping our feet.

"You mean we don't get to work with the women folk?" I said, feigning spit. "That don't wash in Tennessee. Heck, Aunt Jule, Uncle Bob, they met that way. Been married for years. . . they're the same person you know," I said, tucking him under the ribs.

He looked at me as if my head were on backwards, said "Watch out for this one," to Tom, who had just entered the van.

"If Jean-Michel has a problem, let me shake your hand," he said with a huge grin.

"Tainted," I replied, extending my mitt, and soon we were all shuffling over, making room for the late arriving, still stamping our cold feet.

Once we were on the road, I asked Nick what we would do first? "Not to worry. Just follow the crowd. Someone will always be around to direct you. A service of the place, I think," he said flashing his big Ukrainian smile.

"A nice change from the outside world," added Tom. "We'll load up the van for the farm first, then lauds in the chapel. After that, my favorite: breakfast," (he smiled). "Then work. They'll probably send you to the farm. New people usually go there first, something about the healing rhythm of the animals."

Work. I was againest it.

I was going to say something to Nick, but he was back in his Bible again. Everyone was lulled to silence by the sound the cold ground made as it tested the morning tires, as we backed out and onto the main road, the beautiful white countryside opening up around us, freezing exhaust trailing like a small fugitive flag.

At least four inches had fallen overnight; the trees were caked with luffs of snow, and the clear, cold pale blue early morning sky seemed frozen, breakable.

When we got to the main compound, the van backed up to the kitchen door. The guys formed a line, and into the vehicle went cold, empty milk containers, a myriad of plastic buckets, wooden shelf beds for bread, two egg baskets, jugs, and bottles.

An attractive young, aproned woman helped with things on her end. And judging by how cleanly both male and female embraced the new day, the humor that passed between them, I didn't see any strain between the sexes. What had Jean-Michel been talking about?

Once that was completed, Greg, an artist, came around to the front of the van, introduced himself. "Day one, eh? So how do you like the place so far? Has anyone suggested the priesthood yet?" When I said no, he responded. "Just wait, I'm taking bets. We'll keep track. If someone mentions it within three weeks, I win a buck."

"On you like a cheap suit, eh?"

"My mother should be so persistent. Two different people this last week alone." He led, walking away from the house, into a brisk wind, tears forming then running horizontally back from our faces in the wind. Ice began forming on his beard.

"What's up now?" I asked, clapping my deerskin mitts.

"Lauds."

"Does this mean we have to pray. Will people be watching?"

"Probably. . . . Next thing you know, they'll be telling us where to work, what we can eat."

Walking between St. Paracletus and the orchard, we found ourselves joining others as we eventually turned right, past some outhouses, garages, a compost heap, shuffling our feet through the newly fallen snow if we felt like it in the process. At Greg's pace, we passed a bunch of folks, most of whom had smiles, a good word for him.

"Geez, these people seem to actually like you. Have they talked to you yet?"

"They see the collar."

The chapel was mid-sized, beautiful, out in the middle of the woods, evergreens, limited undergrowth on all sides. Made out of huge square logs, coated a darkish rough brown, it was built out of almost as much mortar as wood. Constructed by someone who knew what they were doing, it had a bright golden dome, a Byzantine cross on top. It was simple, with all the elegance that can come with that.

We opened a wooden door with horizontal *fleur-de-lis* metal supports and stepped inside. I was surprised. There were no pews, just a highly polished floor where the younger folk knelt in their socks. Older staff members sat on benches that were built into the walls along the back sides, left and right. Up front was a simple Western altar, with cross-slatted gates and partitioning iconostasis behind it, leading to the Byzantine sanctum, a silver dove hanging from a chain above another altar.

Icons of Mary holding a baby Jesus, and Jesus, full-grown, his sandal strap unfastened, each hung on one of the partitioning walls. Smaller pictures of the apostles dutifully hung alongside those. The pictures, icons, like the chapel itself, were executed by someone who knew what she (I would later find out) was doing.

(Hi, Joan!)

On the left side of the chapel, above a side door was a carved wooden relief of the Infant, in swaddling clothes, with the words underneath: "Lord, give me the heart of a child and the awesome courage to live it out." I was dumbfounded by what I could only call the devotion of all these normal-looking people. Some of the young ones in the middle prostrated themselves on forearms, foreheads, Jean-Michel included.

Others knelt straight up, some sat cross-legged, hands, palms up, at their sides. What was I doing here, I wondered? Insulting Martians, what they believed in, basically. They didn't deserve this, that much was clear, but I didn't want to go back to my small dark room either, to beer bottles, to empty winter walks. I'd just have to try and be respectful, play things off as best I could until I could figure out a next move. Maybe I'd get turned on to something up here, get wind of a good job, become a lumberjack or something.

I had no idea.

Everyone, I noticed, had taken a book of Psalms and a folder of songs from the shelves near the back door. So I retreated, did the same. I slid down next to Greg, who was among those kneeling straight up; he was quiet and rapt, his hands folded in front of him. I sighed, closed my eyes, sitting there, tried to become invisible.

Brought to attention by a tuning pipe, I rose with everyone else, fumbled as they did with my Psalm book as I listened, the singing having begun. Each side of the chapel alternated, sang the basic notes of what must have been Gregorian chant, call and response, like in jazz. But this was something other. The singing was extraordinary in its simplicity; it took me somewhere else. To feeling—but not to me feeling. It was high and lovely. I wondered why I had never heard anything like that before in my life. It made me feel like I was waking up on some new morning turf, surrounded by a fading mist.

It went on for three Psalms, then we sang a few hymns from the folder. These, too, simpler, and yet more complicated than any hymns I'd ever heard before. More haunting notes that moved me to a spiritual reality which seemed to hold things together, that seemed to sing through them. They offered new possibilities, for the duration of that song anyway. The schola, as they were called, led the singing. I edged over closer to them. "Who were these guys?" I wondered.

But then it ended.

A few readings followed, some silent sitting. I wondered if it was time to leave. How would I know when to get up? I grew a little anxious as a few people scurried out of there. The kitchen staff perhaps. But most stayed on, informally visiting the icons. People lined up to stand in front of these wooden pictures, to touch them with their hands or lean into them bodily, foreheads against the paint. It was odd, but quiet and reverent; no one seemed to be putting on a show. No high hair and fancy (weeping) Jimmy Swaggart, PTL TV sets for Jesus the winner—popular during my college years.

Finally, as the numbers dwindled, I felt safe in going outside, in following the others. There were bushes along the sides of the wide dirt road. I could have slipped away before breakfast, ducked out and away, hitched and gotten my clothes, been out of the locale before anybody knew. I might have, too, had Tom and Nick not caught up to me.

Tom was in a great mood. When he laughed, wide, at one of Nick's comments, he threw his arms out playfully, as if all of creation had a part in the grand good way of things. Nick, though, on the other side of me, had by that time moved on to a different subject: Padre Pio and the smell of roses. He had been reading the biography and was into the miracles: the Franciscan standing in the middle of the air during WWII bombing raids, warning away Allied planes; all the Confessional wonders, strange ellipses of time, bilocations: how the priest appeared all over Saint Peter's Square during the beatification of the Little Flower. I nodded my head when the situation called for it, tried to figure out how I could get away from these guys, this place.

By the time I'd made it through the basement and upstairs, I saw men shuffling in and out of the kitchen with trays in their hands, bowls of steaming porridge or yogurt or honey, all of it homemade. (I would later learn that this was one of the men's tasks.)

Most of the tables were full, a priest at the head of each. No escape for me. I might've left again, but one of my house-mates slapped me on the shoulder as he passed, said "Welcome, brother," as if breakfast were cause enough to rejoice.

At the table I chose, the priest was an older fellow with a gray beard, taped old man glasses, a Father Gene. Up there in years and tears I figured, a safe light and harbor, somewhere to duck into the reeds, avoid the holy gab and gunfire. But he was not safe. He was the most focused person I'd ever seen in my life; that became clear the more I watched him during the meal. He was all over what was in front of him, the duty of the moment as I later learned it was called. When he was jamming his bread, that's where he was, listening to someone if they were speaking to him, but his whole consciousness, otherwise, was on the bread, the knife.

The present really mattered to him; it was, after all, where all the goods were. And how many people even try to live like that? Most of us take great pains to *be* distracted – or, like my fear for Judy, that she would become so absorbed in the spiritual significance of each act that she might never unself-consciously be able to live any of them.

I could see some of that then. We either put our jam on, vaguely aware of what we are doing, or else we make the spread-ing such a vast and obvious prayer that we live, abstracted from ourselves. Not this guy. He was doing each little thing well because Ekaterina said it must be so. This apparently selfless attention to detail, to the things around him, was worth a look.

He and everyone at the table were friendly. They listened when I told them my name, how I had heard of the place. (I'd decided to make up a new answer. This time I chose the life of a house painter.)

There was a young woman to my right on the side plank, a man and a woman on the other side, and a server to my left. Topics ranged from fasting to Father Gene's time spent in the RAF as chaplain during the Second World War. It was Lent — new to me — so that was the central concern: the desert of the ordinary (that I could relate to); news about what was going on in the bush would be discussed. Current events, too, came up, usually with a sense of foreboding. Canadian or American politics, the temptation of Christ, spiritual darkness. They would read their own news after dinner on Tuesday nights. A holier Cronkite stood up and delivered it off the page.

Meals were a difficult time, especially at the beginning. I felt trapped until the bell rang, had to put up with the lulls in conversation, all of which I felt were my fault; everyone near the end of the meal with a toothpick in his or her mouth, in his own silence, other tables laughing.

Once I began to loosen up, though, I began to enjoy it, the good humor sometimes approaching rowdiness. That took me awhile. At the beginning I just hung on, felt the pressure of not belonging, the pressure my presence helped create.

Unbearable, really. I creaked with it.

The bell to end the meal came mercifully before a breakdown did on that first day, put an end to my woes. The priests led the closing prayer, the prayer for travelers. And after that, surprise of surprises, more confusion. I really had no idea what to do next, where to go as I got up, followed the cattle through the pens. Ed caught me from the side, told me to meet him outside by the basement door. He said he'd be down in a minute.

I waited as I watched people load the van with buckets, bread trays, others scurry like programmed saints about the compound. "When would the other shoe fall?" I wondered: indoctrination, classes, the wired cap. When would they drill the little holes in my neck, insert the rods? And who was getting what out of this whole deal anyway?

No one had even asked me for any money yet, even though I was eating their food, using their water, not using their plumbing. Only one person, in fact, had even asked me what my last name was. I didn't know what to make of it. Nobody lives this vulnerably, in this kind of poverty, without a reason.

"James, you want to go with Hubert and sand the paths? After you're finished, if there's time, meet me in the basement of Paracletus."

Hubert walked with me to the green sheds next to the main building. There were buckets inside, two big mounds of sand. "This is a pretty easy job. You get to meet some people, figure out your life's work. Pray if you like," he said with a smile. As we filled two buckets of sand each, he continued. "Maybe it would be best if we each took a side. I'll do what needs to be done on the other side of the road. You can do this side, the island. Just sprinkle enough sand for traction wherever you see a shoveled path."

"Who shoveled?"

"Some staffers came out during breakfast."

At first I suspected that he had chosen the easy portion for himself, but then I figured, no, he'd probably choose the hardest, call that humility. I could live with that. And it did seem like a good job. No one over our shoulder telling us what to do every minute.

So I grunted in assent, steeped in brotherly concern, and headed for the bridge — it had metaphorical implications after all: the next rise, high ground, and besides, it might prove useful, another way out of this joint should I need to book my way some sub-lunar ice-capped night, all the available VCRs in a bag, Christians with their insufferable kindnesses, their leaflets, at my heels.

The bridge itself spanned a marshy area, all frozen now, with high grass rising on the left above snow level. To the right, as I made my way across, sprinkling stardust as I went, was the mostly frozen river. An inlet, closer to me, frozen as well, had been shoveled off. It looked like a skating rink.

Once I got across, I noticed a little cabin to the right. It looked out over the Madawaska. A nice spot. An engraved relief in wood over the door, quoting St. Francis said: "God asked me to be a fool the likes of which the world has never seen." Must be the big cheese's cabin. (I found out later that I was right: Ekaternia's.) I was impressed. It wasn't unduly large or luxurious. And I didn't see any outdoor signs of a heater or gas line. Maybe she kept all the gleanings in a Swiss bank account? But I heard she was pretty old. What was she waiting for?

Snow was piled high along the maze of newly shoveled paths on the "island," paths that ran around and between other cabins, to water pumps, to the chapel. At one of the cabins, I ran into a very old woman named Yvonne. She had a thick Belgian accent and was what I would later learn was called a Poustinikki, a hermit of sorts. Thin, oldish skin, blue veins, limpid eyes, curly gray hair, she was dressed in an opened coat that first time I saw her, which she had wrapped around herself on her porch. She was trying to get a squirrel to come for a pine cone she had in her hand. Smiling when she saw me, she eagerly enlisted my help in finding her more of them. I liked the idea, could put down the bucket for a while.

There was an unhurried quality to her that, early on, made me think that what she really needed was some gainful employment, a sense of direction. But the trace of stress in her old facial lines, her calm blue eyes, her thick accent, and movement gave me pause. I began to sense some of the peace she was living in.

She had a holocaust number tattooed on her forearm.

And in a while, partly because of her, I stood in the middle of spacious sunlight, a ridiculous new joy: a smaller bucket in a mittened hand, next to a painted green water pump, the cones I had gathered inside. I was able to watch the channel of blue river more from where I stood, its bright pace between the ice under the clearest bluest sky I had even seen, the smell of evergreens scrubbing up the breezes.

I wanted that job for the rest of my life. (Could I get it? Could I have it?)

My last stop on the island was the chapel. Needing a break, I decided to pop in and take another look around inside. To my surprise, there were a few people still at prayer. One older guy was sitting cross-legged in front of the icon of Christ, and an old woman, along the back, on one of the wall benches, sat looking out a cold, opened window.

As I proceeded with the utmost deliberation, I spotted Hubert coming up the other way on the path, furiously spreading his sand.

"In a bit of a rush, aren't we?" I asked, pausing to breathe in the scent of pine.

"Duty of the moment."

"Whose moment?" He smiled, said perhaps I was right. Maybe he did put too much into things, trying to meet a legalized standard. A subtle form of pride. (Of course, I hadn't meant any such thing. My comment was more one of general suspicion.) I found him funny. "What do you expect to get out of all this anyway?" I asked as I was struck by his desire to please.

"Wow, that's good," he said. Again, he was attributing profound undertones to my grouse. Then he gathered himself, said we needed to go to Paracletus, find Dave.

"Maybe we could split, grab a beer or a jay, say we lost our buckets, broke our crowns or something. That the beer came tumbling after."

"Beer at 10:30. Pretty hard core, my friend."

"Call it a gift."

I had crossed the line. I could see that the moment I spoke, but it was too late. I couldn't take it back.

David was down in the Paracletus basement with some older guy named Tom, both with their shiny metal crosses hanging from their necks. Only some of the people here had these, the staff members. The basement was, not surprisingly, extremely ordered. The two of them were hard at it, sorting used screws, unbending nails. Not what I had hoped for: my ideas of ideal communal farming ran more toward large doses of Moses David: freely dispensed wine, random sex with gorgeous young women – decadence disguised as utopia.

But here was where I was.

I had to admit to myself that there was something admirable, basically good, unassuming about these folks. They were there for you. I couldn't deny that. A kind of surreptitious, subterranean hospitality. They offered you a place at their table, a chance for you to work with them in their lives. Why anyone would put himself at this kind of risk I couldn't say. Who knew what kind of druggie might come through the door?

Before Dave could get us into anything new, the bell rang for tea. And soon guys were piling into the basement, washing their hands, combing their hair. Six or seven of them. A staff guy I hadn't met yet introduced himself to me. Don. Shook my hand. Clear blue eyes – the open face of a man used to working with his hands, finding what he needed there. Made me nervous, so I ducked out toward the outhouses as quickly as I could manage.

Everyone in the compound – similar goings-on were taking place at the farm – gathered in the dining room for bread and water at this time. No jam, honey, tea, or milk was offered. It was Lent, and abstinence was in order. People stood around or sat in groups, talked. Don saw me looking lost there, I guess, lingering around Ekaterina's books, came over.

"Do you know the Bee's work?"

"The Bee?" I asked.

"Yes, Ekaterina. She's our foundress."

"No. I should, I know. But I've been caught up in the academic life. You know how it is. Not much time for spiritual reading. Why is she called the Bee?"

I couldn't feel anything to grab onto with this guy, no sense of what mattered to him, or how to get there. He was a blank with a friendly face. (It was like I was on stage or something, and my straight man was wearing a Noh mask.) What could I play off? How could I go along with the script if there were no directions given? It made me feel naked, and I wasn't keen on sharing my boils.

Was his an assumed pose?

Other staff workers turned out to be much the same. They'd talk to you, about your life, about spirituality, but never about themselves. (Most anyway. Some whom I got a chance to work with for a whole day would open up nicely, and they were real enough. Jim Pasternack!) Maybe this guy was just doing his spiritual job, all the while protecting himself from people who came and went with such regularity. It must've been tough, but, still, I had to protect myself as well, didn't I?

I wasn't sure how long I wanted to stay at this place, but I did know that I wanted to be the one calling my own shots.

"A little boy from Harlem, at Friendship House, gave her the name. Said she had the honey. It just stuck after that."

"No pun intended," I said. He smiled. "She worked in Harlem? No kidding. I bet you couldn't do that today?"

Keep talking, I thought. Keep smiling.

"Oh, no. Actually, we have a prayer house there. The bishop asked us to come. That's how it usually works. A few people set up shop, pray for the city, offer retreats. I spent three years in Whitehorse doing just that. God does great things in little houses."

"Well, it seems he's doing a big one here as well."

I was desperate, trying to keep things on an acceptable spiritual level, trying for happy talk, hoping to slip away before I was discovered.

Just then two women came over, Suzanne and Moccasin. Don introduced us, then receded, slapping me on the back, leaving his hand there for a moment.

"She's something, isn't she?" Suzanne said, looking at Bee's picture on the back of one of her books. "Bigger than life. It takes a lot of courage to live like that."

Suzanne was attractive, wore a bright multi-colored scarf around her hair which she kept pulling down at the sides, as if to reinforce her own sense of personal resolve. Her accent was West Virginia, I learned, as they introduced themselves. She had the aura of someone who had been a success in the outside world, was very charming, went out to greet you as an impressive Southern woman can, with the back of her hand modestly presented.

She had a fine, unfettered smile. Without any obvious pretension, her opened face intelligently beamed your way, letting you know that you had all her good attention. She expected a good interaction. All signs of a healthy ego. Nice, generous.

I learned later that she had been a beauty queen, a Miss Cherry Blossom Festival.

"Heal," I said to myself.

"I suppose you're right," I said. "One of the special ones."

"I liked her little book on Apostolic Farming," Moccasin added. "That's the way to go if you ask me. Live on a farm, raise up some pumpkins, kids."

Suzanne smiled. It was obvious that they had talked about that possibility, family and farming. Moccasin was her own bag of seeds: a little hippyish, with long frizzled hair, glasses. She had laughing gray eyes, wore loose clothes. She had the slightest little bounce to her walk. In the month that followed, you could see how much she loved life with the coy, swirling flip she often gave to her hair, twirling a bit with it. It was action designed more for her benefit than for anybody else's. She delighted in being able to carry on in such a female way, apparently, perhaps finding it humorous that no one had ever called her on her slight excess.

And why would one, really? She was delightful.

She was easy, with her penchant for tea and back to the earth talk. She spoke four languages.

"A harmonica and banjo on the porch," I countered. "A little herb in the garden."

Judging by the shocked look on Moccasin's face, I could feel that I'd done it again. "Just kidding, just kidding," I quickly added.

There was a moment of silence.

"It sounds nice to me," Susanne said, missing the reference. She looked over to Moccasin. "God's will be done."

The bell rang soon enough, and it was back to work. Hubert and I followed Dave back into Paracletus's basement. He helped us find a few good axes, no easy task as many of them had been damaged by guests: blows just under the metal head. "Swinging too furiously," Dave said. He sent us beyond the orchard, to the wood stacks next to the garages.

Curious, nosy as ever, I asked Hubert what was in the garages; and surprisingly, he took the time to show me. Stacks and stacks of boxes. What were these for I wondered? "Clothes to be sorted for the poor," he said. "Stick around for the weather to break, and you might get to help."

"Happy days," I said. "I don't care for work, not really."

The wood split easily in the cold weather. We tossed the pieces over near the piled stacks until we felt like setting the axes down. Then we'd go over and construct a row. Hubert stayed pretty much within himself, so I was free to scheme. How could I blow this pop stand? And where would I go – my question, now having the ring, even to me, of fading issues. I was, although I didn't recognize it at the time, searching for a new orientation, an outlook that would justify my staying there for a while. I could handle this Lent stuff. The women were nice. There was a peaceful feel to the community.

It wasn't like I had anything to get back to.

4

Before I knew it, the noon bell rang, and it was Paracletus all over again. To lunch, and after, to hear Ekaterina talk about God. She was a large woman, of peasant stock it looked like in her loose-fitting cream-colored shift. In her eighties, though one didn't notice that so much when she spoke. Her language was, at times, a little archaic, but it came to us unhurried, with the cumulative power of one who had experienced life. Everyone was rapt — at least for the length of his or her respective attention span; you could see that throughout the dining room. Some people worked toothpicks, first on one side, then the other, thumb and forefinger never leaving the wood. Others would lean back against the metal posts, feet outstretched on the bench if no one else were there. Some, near the end of her talk, despite their good intentions, would start to drift, their heads nodding, or bury themselves deeply in their tabled hands. Some would lean in too far; an elbow would slide off a knee. The head would drop, surprise them. They'd look around, shocked.

Occasionally, one could even hear a brief snore, a catch.

(Perhaps the spiritual directors were taking note!)

I was pretty skeptical that first time but decided to listen anyway. It was the least I could do for the asylum they'd provided, the food. Besides, she'd apparently lived a full life, and all these good folk thought enough about what she had learned to line up, or sit up, and listen, so maybe I might catch a nugget or two.

It seemed an odd jay, hospitality aside. There was no money being made. No outward concern for sex. No reward, at least of a tangible nature. So why did they all come, really? They seemed, right from the beginning, to be the sanest people I had ever met, and yet here they were, devoted to what? Being peasants? Where was the prize in that?

" . . . Christ wears the faces of the poor. We have all heard that before. We hear the sermons every day in the chapel, exhorting us to give a cup of water to the thirsty, and we are sure we would, too, if we were in the middle of things, in Regina (laughter) or in one of the soup kitchens; if it weren't for our daily, some-times hum-drum routines: making bread or chopping wood, trying to be nice to someone who, if the truth be told, is not such a pleasant individual.' (More laughter.)

She smiled for a moment, continued. "We can even picture it: a beaten man, like in the Samaritan story, along the side of the crossroads in downtown Toronto. We would stop and help him to a hospitality house, right in the middle of all the pedestrian traffic, the heart of Christ moving in us. We would struggle with this poor man, with his weight, his smell; we would help him to his feet.

"And some of us, indeed, would; but how many of us would think like a sociologist, the social register first, staff included? . . . What good would my picking him up one time do; what good would my giving him one meal do? . . . I have no food. Would that teach him how to work, how to catch fish, or would it reinforce his dependent habits? Maybe in many cases true charity lies in the other direction? Maybe I should leave him to God? It might just be pride on my part, picking up this man. Pride in every direction. The problem is always me. Besides, I already have responsibilities, duties-of-the-moment that come with those. It would be foolish to expect me to make a halfway house of my home, to ask me to literally pick up every tattered beggar I see . . .

"FOLD THE WINGS OF YOUR INTELLECT, YOU FOLLOW-ERS OF CHRIST. . . . LISTEN TO THE SPIRIT. . . . HE WILL LEAD YOU." (These were words from their Little Mandate.)

"Become poorer because you are beggars at the door of God. Be one with the poor because you ARE one of them, less than they, if the truth be known. You who have been shown much, what have you done? . . . You are the ones being picked up, not them. You are the ones being fed. They are feeding you. If you can't see that, you will lie in your ditch for a long time. Good Samaritans come in all kinds of clothes.

"Reach for the ragged man, crucified on the street, spreading sand, chopping wood. He will feed your need. He is what you can do, what you can repay. He is Christ Jesus, the one who has no place to lay His head.

"We are not poor enough. That is our problem. I look around here, and all I see are rich people in borrowed clothes. People who want meat at meals, people who want insulation in their houses, salt on their tables. . . . Go back to work. . . . Go. . . . You disgust me. There is too much distance between you and that poor man, between you and Christ. You value respectability," she said, raising her cane. "Take it then, into the fields, to the bread ovens, see how far it will get you."

She turned her face.

There was quiet, some rustling. Finally, a few people began to meekly get up, start to go back to work. Then more. She stopped them before the first got to the door.

"Stop! Sit down. . . . How can you reach the heights unless you realize that you are at the bottom? . . ." she asked quietly. After a long pause; "We must stay there. . . . Let me tell you a story. . . . Once, many years ago, Dorothy Day invited me to come to Manhattan to visit her. . . . A prostitute, late in the night, came after me. . . . There was no place to put her, no place for her to sleep. . . . Dorothy did not hesitate. She would sleep between the two of us, on the only bed available.

"Having been a nurse, I wondered if there was such a good idea. The thought of disease, tb, venereal infection, crossed my mind. . . . Dorothy realized my apprehension, looked at me calmly and said, 'Ekaternia, this is the face of Christ.'"

You could've heard a pin drop.

"It's like they say, if you have anything to lose," she said, pounding the table, speaking loudly now, "you must lose it. I had to lose my homeland, my people, Russia. I had to lose Harlem, Toronto, respectability. I was called a Communist because I was from Russia and valued poverty. When we came up here to this little farm in 1947 because the bishop had asked us to, there was nothing here but a broken-down old house. So you know what we did? We planted an orchard. God would, unbeknownst to us, use us as He has always used people, in whatever way that best serves Him. That was all we wanted. Nothing for us. Don't you see? Nothing for you. There is nothing for you. If it doesn't hurt you, it's not love. If part of you resists, there is still sin in you. I repeat: it's not about you, ever, your feelings, your ideas. It's about Him, others. Loving them in Him, in your nothingness, which is Him also. It's about losing who you think you are so that you might become who you were made to be.

"It was God again, in 1947, writing straight with crooked lines. I would be a poustinikki for a while, until my village came. Until you all came. People I never asked for. . . . Like in Russia. Russia people! Every hamlet with a church in the center, a hermit under thatched roof on the outskirts, his door always open. . . . I remember my mother taking me, a child of three, a baroness and her daughter, to visit the bearded ones, the Staretzes. And as we made pilgrimages from shrine to shrine, monastery to monastery, a rich woman and daughter on foot, walking on good Russian sandals, I wondered what it all meant.

"In the night sometimes, my heart longs for that mystery, for those days again, for the Russia of my youth. When Christ was at the center of every town, every community." She stopped here, sunk heavily, unselfconsciously, in her backless chair, and I got a sense that she was somehow bearing the weight of people's sins.

She buried her head in her hands for a moment, her gray hair pulled up on top of her head, braided, bobby-pinned, eventually rising up out of that.

She recovered, gathered herself.

"Baah! What do you have today? Communities like Toronto where neighbors don't even know each other. And television. A pop therapist on every corner. People running in circles, trying to avoid the poor man from Nazareth. How fast do you have to run when you are going nowhere to being with?" She liked that one, twinkled a bit. "Now go, go to work. And work hard. . . . And love yourselves, people, love others. That is what you have to give. If you succeed at the little things . . . smaller ones will follow."

She smiled.

I liked her.

She was rude, didn't care for what anybody said, thought of her. She didn't bow to anybody, or maybe to everybody. In any case, I must admit I felt drawn. She asked for so much, but that was a given in this crowd. What else was worth it? "Could you follow?" she asked. "Did you have enough guts to do it?"

This was unsure ground, a far cry from my college days: Sunday mornings coming down, the Calvinist hair-hats, pompadour Gospel hours (and that was just the men) on TV. I'd sit with my roommates; we'd switch back and forth between those staged amens and big-time small-city rassling, body slams in the common room. They both seemed of a piece in some way. Pure Americana: the complete victory of style over substance – the yea, the crowd, the cathartic heal and physical pay-off.

Everything I wanted out of life, at a quarter the price.

(A theologian friend of mine has since used the expression – "fast-food religion.")

These boys (and girls) in front of me there in Canada, around me, seemed different.

Here was this ornery bird, somehow peasant and aristocrat at the same time, with her simple manner, high, romantic tone, pointing out to me just how shallow I was.

The nerve!

In the words of Kris Kristofferson, she'd been reading my mail.

Might as well check it out since I was stuck up there in the woods.

Maybe this poor dead guy was calling me through the ruins of time.

In any case, it was hard to argue with sense.

For a moment I drifted back to my youth, to my Aunt Amelia in Denver, that picture of my favorite, the Little Flower, on her wall. My mom's sister used to say her beads, walking around the house, me under her dining room table.

(I later remembered that I had asked her to pray to the flower lady for me.)

I wondered how Amelia was doing, decided to write her. . . .

Someone rang a bell. Lunch was over.

Hey, I wasn't finished. I wanted to lift that little sucker — though how would I find the thing? There was a whole collection of them, some painted, some silver, perched beneath the photos behind Ekaterina's backless perch as I passed her table. (She was talking to a female guest.) There were pictures of her with Cardinals, an old Pope, with John Howard Griffin, I would later learn, the author of *Black Like Me*, her head on his chest. There was one with her recently deceased husband, two with her old Harlem House friends, Claude McKay and Thomas Merton.

She'd been around for a long time.

"How come I'd never heard of her?" I wondered. Had Morley Safer been neglecting his duties on *60 Minutes* or what?

I felt like one of the herd again, made moo sounds, garnered a few smiles as I drifted with the masses, all of us heading down the stairs. Maybe I'd go to the farm that afternoon, I thought. That might be interesting.

Jean-Michel cut me off.

"Hey, grizzled American, don't you know it's half-day today? What are you up to?" I must've looked puzzled. "Didn't anyone tell you? We have the rest of the day relatively free, until vespers. Are you going to get that coat? . . . Hello," he said, as if knocking on my head.

"Let's hitch out of here," I suggested.

He rolled his eyes. "St. Joseph Center. Come on, I'll walk you up. I want to stop at the restaurant, get some real food. . . . You interested?"

"Yes, yes, lead on, MacDuff!"

We headed up the road.

About halfway up toward the thrift store, we were passed on the other side by two young women crunching in the same direction. "Josie and Clare," he said immediately, yelling a friendly hello, his breath before him. They responded in kind, but neither he nor they made any attempt to cross the road and talk. Very un-Jean-Michel like it seemed to me.

"Not allowed . . . we'd need a staff member with us. . . . Can you believe that? They're wary of scandals among the locals. Tea's about the only time, though it's not uncommon for a staff member to come over and join your little soiree if you exhibit questionable behavior."

"Which would include what?"

"Talking."

The girls turned up an overgrown rural road to the left.

"So they have no rutting festivals in the spring, then; we don't get to wear horns, paint our faces blue, do goat dances?"

"Well, you can. I think there's a place over there in the woods. . . . But they won't. They're celibate."

"Hey, I like vegetables . . ."

"Tennessee, right?"

I threw my arm over his shoulder, gave him a hearty squeeze. "I like you. . . . You're French. . . . Well, I guess, when in Rome. . . . It's an odd world all the way around, don't you think?"

"Here, anyway."

St. Joseph's Center, the rural apostolate, was your basic large scale garage sale. Everything from children's books to old work boots. Staff members ran the place, Janine and Mary Kay. More cars were parked around the place than I thought were in the vicinity. The lot was filled; there were cars lining the grass on both sides of the lesser road we'd walked up on, creating a limited corridor to drive through. The locals had descended with a vengeance.

Things ran smoothly. There was order, if not space, shoes divided by type, coats by size, color. We were even offered a cup of orange pekoe tea. Donated.

The community lived out the words of their foundress: they got on quite well with the neighbors. In order to hit Morley Safer and *60 Minutes*, you needed to get the locals in a huff; we needed some paranoid folks, a few AK-47s, general redneck-ery.

I found a good coat, a hat, gloves, all for three funny dollars, a few of them thin questionable Canadian courters. Left my borrowed clothes. I wanted to mill about some, but Jean-Michel was anxious for faster food. And he wasn't alone: before the restaurant door down the road had finished ringing its bell to greet us, Nick and Tom, already at table, invited us over, several female guests at a different, distant table. Our two mates were busy nursing strawberry milkshakes, said they'd skipped lunch for this opportunity.

Taking off our gloves, hats, we sat down. Jean-Michel said he was giving up Lent for Lent, the ultimate sacrifice, but ordered only fries with his shake. I went the whole nine yards, ordered two cheeseburgers, fries, a barrel coke.

"It's Wednesday and you're ordering meat?" Nick asked.

"I'm not into Lent," I replied, figuring that if I wasn't among friends, at least I wasn't among enemies. Jean-Michel laughed; the others just looked at each other. Tom's mouth falling open.

"Well, I'm not a Catholic," I added.

"Yet," Nick smiled, good humor in his eyes.

Tom was elsewhere. "I'm afraid I'm not totally used to all of that good farm food yet. I guess I needed some sugar," he confessed.

"Talk to Fr. Pelton," joked JM.

"Skipping lunch makes it even, don't you think?" asked Nick.

"This adds a little mid-week spice for me. . . . Just this once. Besides, we don't want to get legalistic about things, do we?" an engaging smile spreading across his face.

The waitress brought our drinks, smiling, asked Tom and Nick if they needed anything else.

Jean-Michel and I just looked at each other.

"Well, frankly, I could use a little female companionship," he said after she'd left.

"I don't know if I agree," Tom said. "This is a place for serious interior work. If the Lord has someone in mind for you, you'll meet her at the right time."

"Jean-Michel has a vocation," joked Nick. Everyone laughed.

"I suppose that's true, though I think I need to do a thorough search before I jump into anything."

"So James, you're from Cleveland?" Nick asked.

"My last stop," I said, immediately turning the conversation. "So tell me, why are you so up all the time, if I can ask? I've never seen anybody smile that much who wasn't up to something."

Nick enjoyed spiritual conversation.

"Joy of the Lord, gratitude . . . though I don't want to take credit for anything," he said. "God is so good. I went through so much of my life without even realizing how much is possible. . . Joy. . . It's the fruit of the Spirit." And then to make sure he didn't sound too pious, he added. "Watch it, I might start dancing on the table!"

"Please not that Charismatic stuff again," said JM.

"Well, I for one would like to hear more about it," Tom said, as the man from Mon-re-al starting to loll his tongue around like Linda Blair from *The Exorcist*.

Nick remained relatively discreet.

"Father Pelton says they're going to do a Life in the Spirit sometime this spring. So the opportunity might come up."

"No thanks," Jean-Michel concluded.

The volleys continued. Finally, after we'd all had enough of water and refills, we headed back. I walked alone, behind in the cold, needed to think about what Nick has said. He seemed like he had his head on straight; so why was he talking this gratitude nonsense? Self-hypnosis? What in the larger world was their worth feeling grateful for: war, famine, the violence inside of us, inside of God?

There was still time before vespers when I got back, so I ambled around in the basement, looking for something to do. The ping-pong table was being used; someone was on the piano, another person trying hard to accompany the latter on guitar. It was pleasant to lean against a bookshelf for a few moments, to listen; but I got restless, went outside.

I hadn't seen the front of the house yet, so I walked around to my left after I came up from the basement. A little path led me past a very unusual statue of Mary. It was as if she were flying: bluish, coppery, her veil blown back, her arms outstretched. As if she were coldly, mysteriously coming for each devotee.

There was a nice view out front, lawn chairs, covered in snow, a nice view of the Madawaska. It was still very cold. You could hear the occasional loud crack of river ice some mornings, still see smoke out over the water, the air colder than the river. It couldn't have been any more than ten degrees out there, a cold snap some at lunch had said.

It was at this point that I heard people carrying on over to the left, so I followed the noise to the inlet on the riverside of the small bridge. Guests and staff had lined up barrels on either side of the shoveled outdoor rink. Two per side, the inside space being the goal area. Contestants were armed with brooms so old that they were without yellow straw below the sewn threads. It was hockey on ice, played in boots, no skates. It looked like great fun, what with the high banks serving as boards.

The pace was civil; no one got blasted, though some did meet the weather conditions face to face (momentarily). I stood on the sidelines, enjoyed the futility of the game. Daoud noticed me first, waved me over enthusiastically, said their side needed all the help they could get. I did okay at high school baseball, but had never been one for violent sport; it had always seemed too fascist a deal: win one for the dead zombie, the Gripper.

That kind of thing. But this was big fun because everyone was inept out there. Everybody looked ridiculous. If your feet or the ice didn't trip you up, a house mate would.

I liked the concept. So I played, would try to run, my cartoon feet going much faster than I could. I couldn't control direction or pace either, couldn't stop. People comically took to saying hello and goodbye whenever anybody slid by, out of control, everyone getting good and sweaty with the wasted effort.

Vespers came too soon. I wanted to keep on playing, lay there on the bank, my cherry cheeks, wet and cold, my hot breath and good sweat, heavy breathing. But there was such cheer in the winding down that I happily went with the flow, felt my face and feet burn as I warmed up in the chapel.

There was a chalice on a small back table this time. People put hosts in as they entered. And once again, that music, simple, where the heart is, rising to God's low, deep own, if He was and had one. I was moved by the simple faith of these people. They weren't perfect; I knew that. I'd already seen some of their flaws. But they were honestly confronting their condition, without the frills, at least what they assessed it to be. That was admirable. And they seemed to be prospering personally, if not financially, in what they were doing.

Of course, if all of this did anyone any good out in the real world was another question. Maybe they figured that we, the few, the proud, could take some of it back, bring about a sea swell of change. Convenient, then, this cold oasis? Maybe. But it wasn't easy; they had to show up every day, not collect their pay.

Any reservations I had were swallowed up in the Mass that followed, at least for a time. I had always seen ritual as a hollow hope, if the only one some people had. That was pale recommendation enough for me, in a world that offered little otherwise. Whatever got one through the night. But I was amazed at this service.

The priest, a Father Wild, spoke from another place: unashamed, holy it seemed, patient in being there. When he said, "Let us pray," he meant it, would move back deeply inside himself, a place where he obviously spent a great deal of time, his whole presence somehow filled with light. Slow, illumined, he'd rock and forth behind the altar; and when he gave his sermon, he spoke from a mutual, simple place, common to all of them. All of them at home in what he called "the desert of the ordinary."

It was by me, this gratitude in picking up a needle, in the splitting of logs. I didn't get it. The One who becomes more, he said, as we become less. None of them seemed to have suffered from the transition. That much was clear.

I didn't know what to think. And then when he raised the Host, he left us for a while. I don't know how else to put it. The simple bright peace on his face said enough, him vacationing, just he and Some Other. I tried to blend in with those seated as people formed two lines to go up and get fueled. Ekaterina appeared from the left. I hadn't even noticed her there though she was wearing a bright stocky red dress with colorful beaded embroidery about the neck.

There was something special about her, I couldn't deny it. A bright presence, an aura of real power, spiritual power. I actually felt repelled by its force as she passed in front of me on her way up.

I was going to join in the procession, fake my way through, just to make it appear as if I belonged, but that didn't seem right after seeing her there. This was serious business to these folks. I didn't want to walk on that. I also knew that in not doing so I would mark myself (like the reluctant parishioners in *The Pardoner's Tale*) as one who needed counsel.

Well, that had never been a secret.

Noh-dinner was bread and tea. Lent again. I wondered how long this would go on. Hand me my whip, discipline, like they talked about at the dorm: "Thank You, Jesus. May I have another?" What was the point of all this I wondered, nibbling on my bread. Would this make them holy or remind them that they were not? Why not at least eat when considering the possibilities?

Afterwards, there was the chore known as "vegetables" in the basement below the kitchen. All the men guests would stand around pails of water and peel, shave, cut anything plant-like that needed to be so dealt with. There was always much conviviality. Sex was never discussed; sports, hardly ever. But there was no shortage of conversation. Papal encyclicals, politics around the world, personal playful slurs, banter on the subject of vocation (Greg wincing).

The visiting priests pitched right in with the rest of us, someone in the kitchen dropping down to make suggestions if those were needed. Those were followed without fuss. People, busy in relative harmony; self-seeking taking, at least from all appearances, second place for a moment. I wondered what I would have to do to jump into the middle of this, become part of it, instead of just sitting back on the periphery like I had always done. I could become a Catholic again, take that bread.

I didn't know yet, but decided to just keep saying the right things, listen hard; I could learn from these people.

Things were changing for me – even then I could hear it.

(I sounded like Judy!)

My situation would eventually become as clear as those bright yellow buckets. The longer I stayed with them, the more I understood. Basically, I would rather be like them than like me. There was a light there; purpose, and, even if I didn't see it initially, slowly, through the months, I was beginning to turn, gratefully, to meet it.

Evenings were a time for backgammon, reading, visiting, or going to classes when they had them. Sometimes there would be staff meetings, at other times the "Bee" would meet with the working guests in a big room upstairs, answer questions, relay her past. (Once she read my soul in a very specific way. The two of us were at a dining room table talking, and she leaned back a little, dramatically circled her breast with one of her hands. Both the orphan and the lustful young man exposed. Extraordinary stuff.)

Evenings were a pleasant time, all in all, though you couldn't call them a break from the day. There was none of that, except for the times when a visiting priest would pile in with us in one of the guest's cars, hotfoot it over to Ottawa or to Barry's Bay for a beer, some 8-Ball vocation talk on a Wednesday evening.

On one of my first evenings, I spent some time with Clare, a beautiful mostly French-speaking girl from Quebec. The bluest eyes, deep cut lines between cheek and mouth, smooth skin. She was practicing her English on me, and I was getting along rather well until Dave came over, asked to talk to me in the smaller Madawaska-facing front room.

Nice place: windows, books, magazine racks, a phonograph.

He said, as we sat alone at the long table in there, that he was concerned about the drug thing. Had I been taking them before I came up? How long was I off them — was that the case? They'd had bad experiences in the past with LSD and needed to be cautious. I was as forthright as I dared to be (not at all), with respect, because I was just beginning to like the place and didn't want to leave. I told him about Conurbation, my discomfort; about how I moved to Cleveland, and with the help of grace, had started grad school in English. And the dope, just a few harmless tokes with fellow students at a party one night. I told him it gave me a headache, that I hadn't inhaled. The whole experience had made me a little paranoid, to be honest. I felt like I needed to sit in a closet.

God had taken me through all that.

He sat back, rubbed his chin. After a very pregnant pause, we prayed together. When he came back, he said he'd be willing to let it go, reluctantly. But if I had any problems with my past, though, I should seek him out or a priest or the staff doctor.

Then he switched gears, asked me who I liked poetry-wise. Hopkins, definitely. Did I like Alice Meynell, Belloc, Chesterton, "The Hound of Heaven," Thompson's latinate approach? And what about fiction? Dostoevsky? Tolstoy? What about Mauriac, Bernanos, Waugh? I said I'd put them on my list, that I had most recently been reading some deep-image people:

Bly, Wright, Merwin, Kinnell. Then I threw in a few Field translation names, just to make me sound more convincing: Vasko Popa, Gunter Eich.

Before I could edge away, he suggested that I find a spiritual director, a guide.

Jean-Michel greeted me as I came out. "The third degree, eh?"

"How was I supposed to know that she was fifteen?"

The bell rang and the nightly song ensued.

I'd actually picked up a few words, eyes closed. When we got back to the dorm, though, I made it a point not to speak to anyone, went right to bed.

5

As we rolled toward Easter, I finally got my chance to spend some consecutive days on the farm. Janine, a different one, drove the van out after loading. It was about five miles out to St. Benedict's Acres. On the way there the first day, we slowed down to salute one of the visiting priests who was taking a brisk hike from his priestly residence at Carmel Hill—it was even farther out in the boonies—to the Main House. For health reasons. After we passed him, someone mentioned his life in Eastern Europe under the Communists before he had been smuggled out: prison, torture, starvation.

Whiner.

An extremely short fellow came out of the back door of the farmhouse to greet us, tuque in hand, as we got out of the van. He was youngish, in his 30s, monastic-looking with his naturally balding head, short hair, ready smile. Richard was his name.

Before I could voice a preference (one never did), I was out chopping wood again in what felt like zero-degree weather. Surprisingly enough, the conditions were manageable, at least once you'd figured out how to cope. Jumping up and down on my toes until I could feel them always worked for me. Once I'd gotten that far, I'd be good for the whole morning. But then I had to deal with the wood pile thing again. The constant repetition of the place was getting to me.

I got set up between an outhouse and an aluminum corrugated half-moon-shaped building which was filled with horse harnesses, tools, all the merciless physical details of farm life. And though I tried to amuse myself by measuring the relative effectiveness of my strokes, how hard a swing it would take to split what kind of log, the whole thing bored me to frozen tears. There was no getting around it: the "ordinary" could be staggeringly painful, boring. So, resourceless, like Henry, I'd stop, sit down on the logs, see how far I could spit in the snow, look out over the horizon, clap my deerskin mitts at the trees, listen for the echo.

The hills across the way offered some consolation. The trees looked frosted, like earthen bristles, covered as they were with snow. But even that didn't last. Chop, chop, stack, stack, take this monkey off my back. Try as I might, I couldn't do much to keep my mind off of my predicament. I even tried making angels in the snow. What kind of life was this anyway, I wondered, out chopping wood with no visible means of support, except these puppet wires, and me, 24 and strong, lame as I could be? If God was so real, why couldn't He at least be interesting? Give me a life, some bourbon walnut fudge, liqueur-flavored chocolate balls?

A big part of me wanted to bury that ax in corrugated tin, to take off through the fictional trees, find some wolves, bear grease, night fires. I could learn grunting behaviors, smear the entrails of animals all over myself inside a large circle. I could hunt beasts with a knife. At least that would be living. Druidic and stupid, but living. Not this barter-my-time-for-bread-and routine routine.

But before I got farther into my grouse, I was interrupted by singing. It started from the upstairs of the little farmhouse. About sixty yards away. Farmers praying. And it came to me: this was it for these guys. There would be no Hollywood Bowl, no short tight skirts, no Bentleys. And it became clear, too, that they had chosen the harder part. This wasn't an escape from the outside for them, but a more difficult way into the middle of it. What could you run away from here, after all? You couldn't hide beneath your latest jag. There were no jags to be had. Here you had to get up the next morning and do the same stupid thing you did the morning before for years at a time or until someone gave you a different, impossibly ordinary job.

It would have driven me up the complete wall. And, yet, there they were, singing through it. Happier than clams, or at least they seemed to be; happier than anybody I had ever known.

Father Pelton talked after lunch about service, freedom, the God of the ordinary. "We are called to use every minute to grow during the difficult days; we are called to allow ourselves to be cracked open by Love.

"And what will we be left with? Joy. An unrestrained joy. . . . And then we will look around one day, without ever having thought about it, and we will be holy. We will be friends of God.

"It's like Ekaterina says, 'Come up higher. . . . Love, love, love, never count the cost.' Move in that Love, if you feel it or not. Move in Nazareth, transformed, in the ordinary which has never been so. . . . This is our part."

When I went back to work, I thought about what I had caught there. Holiness. Dude! Was that what all of this was about? What about my writing deal? What about Buffy, my home in Malibu?

All jags, to prove I was alive; no secret there.

And while I knew, too, that I didn't want to spend the rest of my life in trying to get a gold-er cup, the perfect looking female appendage, I still had to wonder, what was worth pursuing?

The next step.

I mean, that's all I had.

Somebody got me onto reading *Brothers Karamazov.*

I liked it, but I couldn't—and still—can't buy Alyosha. The guy's too clean, too pure. It's like original sin never made the trip. (And thus the Orthodox take on that is refuted. Even as an old man, I've never met a person without sin; everyone sins too much every day. Jesus by nature, Mary by grace. Nobody else. There are people who call themselves godly, but I have trouble buying that.)

Speaking of sin, as I moved my spotted way through Lent, I spent more and more time on the farm. With (Dear) David (Fr. David, now, with Parkinson's as I write this), a staff member, I helped make yogurt and cheese. At other times I held sheep by the scruff of their neck as someone delivered the clean hole through their foreheads. We hung 'em high, cowboys, upside down while their guts flopped, as Whitman put it, horribly into the pail.

I had to learn how to skin them, punch my fists between skin and muscle, try to separate the two, rip down the pelts like the unwanted portions of our lives.

I'd go to the cross at the top of the hill during tea sometimes, for the solitude. Not to pray, but just to look around. Was the loneliness I felt like Jesus's? Maybe to some degree, though I wasn't here to save anyone; that much was clear. At the time, I felt like I needed a woman, some concurrent action. It was too tough a sledding, that place. There was no comforting insanity. No chance to run naked through the forest, ram my head into a tree, just to taste my own cranial juices; no opportunity to get blasted, no chance to count the frigging stars.

So when I found out that Tom/Adam knew some guy in Denver who could get me some good paying construction-type work, I was ready to move.

But I had to balk at leaving that first time.

Amelia lived out that way, but she wouldn't be enough. Within a week, I'd run into too much of the ordinary – and then what would I do? I'd start reeling again, end up in a drunk tank.

I needed a reason to push, a goal, some granite to stand on. What the heck did I want out of life anyway, and what was I willing to do to get it? I still had no idea. As I brooded over my fate one evening, I saw Fr. Pelton sitting over by himself, reading a magazine.

I had to talk to somebody.

He was kind. I had to give him that, right off the bat. Smiling, he offered a quiet place upstairs. I followed him up a very narrow set of stairs to a tiny room above the kitchen: his bedroom apparently, with small cot, pictures of Mary, crucifixes on the wall. I told him what I could, more than I had anyone else. He seemed concerned, but untroubled. Was I in any trouble? Was I on the lam? (A bit of a poet himself, he liked the expression.)

He asked about the state of my soul. I said I didn't know if I had one. "Do you believe at all?" he asked. I said I was struggling with everything, told him that sometimes I felt like a bubble in a tar pit. At that point he rose from his chair, quickly, but without hurrying, placed his hands on my head.

I was shocked, didn't know what to do or say. He began praying earnestly, spontaneously to this Jesus guy. He asked that I be helped in finding my way, that I allow the light that had drawn me here to enter completely, to change me. And then, just as abruptly, he stopped.

I left after some further talk, told him that, yes, I'd see him the next week. Try to relax, he told me; live the days, pray as best I can. And as I walked down the stairs, pictures all along the close walls, I wondered just what had happened here. I felt different in some way, lighter in my step, almost dizzy. Well, none of this could do me any harm, that much was certain. I slept better than I had in a long time that night, got up the next day to joyfully sort potatoes at the farm with Hubert. Large ones from the small.

Sounds innocent enough, but after a while the line becomes blurred. What exactly constitutes a small potato, what, a large? Hubert and I agreed that life was like that. The more you tried to analyze anything, the more you sank into the slough of despond.

And yet how could one not do so?

"The rational mind isn't worth all that much, I think, at least when it comes to the important stuff," he said.

"You sound like my ex-girl. She was into Native American and flower essences."

116

He smiled. Apparently not unfamiliar territory.

"I guess you're right. You've got to be able to separate things, but what does Kat say, 'Fold the wings of your intellect.'" (He said this grandly, self-consciously.)

"Joke number two!"

He smiled.

"I just want to be faithful. What else matters? . . . It's the flesh we wrestle with. How do we get past these surface considerations? How can we immerse ourselves in prayer, become prayer? That's the tough question, if you ask me. There are no easy answers when it comes to the daily stuff. You just have to work through it. . . . I'm glad I'm here in any case. It's a great blessing, don't you think? To be given time and a place to find out who you really are, to find out how to live your life? That's why I came, anyway."

"I came for the girls."

"Oh, come on. Hasn't this place had an effect?"

"Yeah, maybe too much. I'm thinking of becoming a nun."

"And that's bad? You've been out there. You know what it's like. It gets inside you. . . . We're all sinners to begin with, and to end with, but I want to be ready."

"Good luck with that."

"Yeah, I know. But I want all I can get. You going to sign up for the Charismatic Renewal class? Should be coming around pretty soon."

"I don't know. Could be a spiritual doobie."

"Maybe. . . but maybe not."

We climbed, in our mutual squats, up one mound and down the other, (we had a time, oh, brother) dragging out bushel baskets behind us (setting the woods on fire).

When I next saw Fr. Pelton I asked him about this born-again business.

He said that there were many twice-born people, but many once-born people, too, people who have been faithful since childhood. A decision, or, as he said he liked to put it, a movement or realization usually seems to happen somewhere along the line for all of us though. He said he didn't think it had to be a dramatic thing. For him, in fact, it was just a gradual realization that Jesus was the way things truly were. How could he say no to what was so patently obvious? And he didn't have to shout out a yes to the world either. That would be looking at a mountain, saying "Yes, you are mountain."

Ridiculous, absurd.

Conversion, he said, meant a "turning," and that's what it is, all of your life. You turn until you become who you are, and then you are in the arms of God. This side of earthly life or the other. . . it didn't matter much ultimately. We are like flowers, coming up and out through the green moss, the dross of sin.

He recommended that I pray to Mother Mary, do an act of consecration, ask her to show me her Son. Persevere. Don't worry. The Lord had brought me this far. He wouldn't let me slip through His fingers. Then he asked me about my family.

I picked up some Lowell: *Land of Unlikeness* and some Margaret Avison. Density seemed its own goal for both in some way, but I liked them.

Good Friday came with a procession and influx of people, all of us going to a special, longer than usual prayer service. We went up to kiss the feet of the Crucified One, a big cross someone held. I felt odd, a bit put off. Who was this guy, really, that I should give my life to Him? God? (In some film Woody Allen, as he sees a revered guru being ushered on his way, muses on the idea of God going to the toilet.)

Jesus. . . was He the place and person where the divine miraculously broke through and into the stained-glass physicality of the world, all in a collection of broken bone and skin?

"For God so loved the world."

It was a wonderful story, one that should be true if it weren't. Weird enough, perhaps. to be so.

I looked at the people around me. They were here for the long haul, because they believed in what they were doing to the point of giving up their lives for it. They found what they needed, were hungrily satisfied, even happy, or as happy as people can be. And they weren't stupid.

I had to check this out.

On Holy Saturday evening there was more prayer, all of us stooping in procession under a black cloth that two people held in chapel. We were going through death with Christ to rise with Him, embracing death. (Nothing new there.) And why not do that here, now, I figured? It seemed healthy in some way.

There was something bare, pleasingly bald about the ritual. It struck me that this was where life was, in Nazareth. These people were truly living. And dying. Not running from life in sleek cars, dope, the hep-est tennis shoes.

Easter was the biggest doings, several lambs (the ones we) killed and mounted especially for the occasion, an apple in their mouths. Innocence, slain. Something that they did every day at the Eucharistic banquet. I had to fit my mind into the idea: this was actually God they were eating each day (God-food), the One who could not sink low enough for us, becoming even literal food.

That was the rap – and why wouldn't it be true? If there was a God, and if He truly loved us, wouldn't He do as much, more than we could for each other?

I kind of dug these Catholics. They were about as far away from the world as one could get – and still be on the planet. But there was something nice about the way they proceeded. They loved, embraced irony, all of it. The sentence contradicted before completed. Not in a deconstructed way, but in a way that acknowledged Absolute Truth and the fact that they could not entirely live It, nor embrace It. They took delight in life, in the mystery and tension of God working out His plan in a time-bound natural world. A world filled with knuckleheads, beautiful knuckleheads like they knew they were.

There were guests from all over the world by afternoon tea.

Colorfully attired, they sang their songs, sometimes spontaneously, did their dances. I saw instruments I could not name, languages I could not understand. It almost made me want to thank God for the first time. (It was very sweet.) To thank Him for bringing me here, to all these lovely foreign smiles; for His having patience with me.

At dinner I sat with Nick and Tom. Tom brought up the renewal, and Nick along with two female guests from Akron began talking about Jesus as if they were all best pals or something. Struck me as odd.

"This is the Charismatic stuff, isn't it? You guys have Him over for bridge?"

They laughed.

"Does He like cards?" one asked the other. Both girls laughed, but I felt put-off. Did they have to have something I didn't? Why did this spirit stuff make them feel so special, set apart?

Was this what it was all about, I wondered? To get to a superior place, a height you could look down from?

(The answer here, for everyone concerned, is always yes. Every Christian does it to some extent. It's called need. We need to be loved and cling to the wrong self until that very last minute – when God pries the stinking idol out of our lying/dying fingers. Francis de Sales summed it up nicely when he said that our pride dies fifteen minutes after we do.)

How tenuous all this looked as I sat in my good communal cage on that evening, looked out at all those smiling, beaming faces.

When we got back to the dorm late that night, later than usual, I found myself pouring over a borrowed Bible with everyone else, the Gospel of John. Each in his own bed. Even Jean-Michel had broken his out. For me it was a kind of greed, the kind Paul recommends. It had become clear to me that I was a fallen creature. (Why it took me so long to figure that one out was perhaps the greatest mystery here!) And if there were spiritual gifts to get, if I could somehow feel more completed through all of this, like Hubert, I wanted every bit of what was available.

Nick reminded us that the Life in the Spirit course would begin a week before Pentecost.

Ascension came and went, as it had in time. And though I finally managed to gird my loins and go to Confession for the first time since I was a small boy, I couldn't help but wonder why Christ had abandoned us. Was it necessary that we play out these perilous times when the battle had already been joined, won? We would have been so much happier had He stayed. Maybe He left so we could share in the victory. So that we could have a chance to fail and therefore be able to live life to its fullest intensity?

Heck, I'd be willing to forego a little freedom just to enjoy the rewards, avoid the possibility of that ultimate failure. In a sermon, Fr. Tom said that God treats us like adults. We would not be happy had we a lesser part. He said it was only in standing up that we could be counted. We are free to fail, and will, repeatedly. But God will not, and that was the important thing. He said we are called to live in His strength, through our paltry wills. Our lives would not be worth living if that were not the case.

So I signed up for the class, waited for some o' that "old time religion" while I washed tea time cups, while I sat at Ekaterina's feet, listening, drifting. And it was fitting preparation. Waiting is our lot in large part, is it not? We try to work hard, but, like all the conscripted, we spend most of our time in lines of one sort or another.

"Power," said Fr. Timothy. "The glamour of it. That's what we find every time we turn on the tube. Elected officials are after it, the few with integrity notwithstanding, which is why so little ever gets done. (Laughter . . . low hanging fruit.) People in the world give up their lives to get some of it. And for what? Some immediate gratification, for an idol that crumbles in your hands.

"Most of us in this room have, at some point or other in our lives, fallen for that lie. (My only problem today is with the word 'most.') We see it every day in our personal relationships.

Yes," he smiled, "even around here . . . though they are celibate relationships." (More laughter). "You'll see it in the larger Charismatic Renewal as well. . . . He with the most gifts, wins. . . . But this is no panacea. Heaven is not yet." An "amen, walls," from the back. "Speak it, brother."

He smiled.

"That's not God's way. We all know that. And it's God's way we are after, are we not?"

Spontaneous clapping — never heard that before.

"We are all here to get what God wants to give us. If there is a speck that we might have missed, or if all this is new to us, it doesn't matter. For how else can we please Him other than in coming to Him? And He will respond, that I can promise you.

"Be warned, though. That response will come in power. Not as the world gives. Let me make that clear. This power is greater. You may see the dead raised, the paralytic walk. You may find yourself speaking a new language. These things testify to the greatness of our God, and we praise Him for it. But don't be confused. The greatest gift anyone can get out of this seminar is a closer walk, a clearer knowledge of who Jesus is, how terribly much He loves him or her. If one person gets moved in some profounder way, if just one fence-sitter becomes filled with fire, then I will feel like our efforts will have been worth it."

It struck me as a bit showy: Earnest Angley, *The 700 Club* with Ben Kinchlow (whom I always liked). Dude sounded a bit like a pitch man. On the other hand, I was there with people I trusted, so I decided not to worry. Besides, it would be kind of fitting if the Lord used a salesman to turn my life around. "The Lord asked me to be a fool, the likes of which . . ."

I looked over to Greg, and he just rolled his eyes, motioned his head toward the door behind us, starting skooching his seated self in that direction. But he knew, as well as I did, that leaving in the middle would have been bad form in this place. (And they had been awfully nice with the food thing.)

As the meetings progressed that week, I found myself, like everyone else there, praying over people. I didn't know really what to make of it. There was jive potential, so I remained distant. There were night sessions of inner healing, scripture study. It was enlightening and good, but, still, I wasn't buying the whole package. (I just wanted an island, not scuba lessons, an umbrella in my mai tai.) I didn't want to end up selling Bibles on the street, embarrassing my old college friends, calling them out as sinners as they passed.

I tried to take the spiritual bath, cleanse myself, when it was my turn to be prayed over. I relayed my sins, though no one had asked for that. Some people were genuinely shocked; some of the guys even looked at me a little strangely in the dorm. (No Carlos Castaneda/dance of the mushroom people fans there.)

But good came of it. Lots of people started sharing deeper stuff. (My T-group shrink back at my first college might have flashed his fake smile in approval!)

It made us all feel closer, gave us a greater affection for each other.

The target day for the Baptism of the Holy Spirit was Saturday, the day before the Old Testament harvest festival, Pentecost. And it couldn't arrive soon enough. My anxiety level began to rise, even as I worried about that. Would it create problems, would it help? Would I get in the way of the Spirit acting (out)? Now that was something I had some experience with.

The plan was for each of us, the ones-to-be-anointed, to meet at a pre-arranged time in the chapel. A team of veterans would pray over each of us. I was to be one of the first.

Before the large icon of Jesus, his sandal strap unfastened— an invitation for those who would be more than John the Baptists—between my new staff friends, I knelt, and after some initial conversation, felt Fr. Pelton and two staff members lay hands on my head. They insisted that I praise the Lord with them whether I felt so moved or not. I did, but it seemed strange. There I was, after all, praying to some guy I wasn't even sure existed, thanking Him for what He would come back from the dead to do in my life, there, in the boonies of Canada.

I felt foolish, but continued, mostly because I had come this far, but partly, too, because I wanted the wholeness it seemed to offer. "Thank You, Jesus," I said, then said again – and then said again. I said it until my jaws literally ached.

But nothing was happening.

(I wondered what Donny and Carp would've said.)

Then, finally, there's no other way to say this, things did. I felt something, a light, something I had never known before: joy began to slowly rise up inside me, a joy that I didn't know was possible for humans. And as that unfolded, the darkness, the gloom, the weight that I had been wrestling with ever since the day I could remember, began to slowly, surely, dissipate; or, rather, it was slowly burnt away, eclipsed by the coming of what would reveal Itself as a complete interior light.

Effusive fountains of light, great handfuls of pearled praise-water gushed up, welled over. My spirit, for the first time in my life, began to twinkle. It began to dance in foreign provinces, in vales of joy; quivering in hundreds of little sunlit beads, each with my face in it, each rising, gelatinous, testing its own impossible shape; the mutating curves of my life, reshaping windows of light, now falling with a splash into the pool with its brothers beneath. All the chaotic motions, sparkling against a little kid's feet, rising up again to meet the descending next in line – in complete sunlight.

All without the birds of denial, nothing but a fresh clear bell of blue sky, possibility, above. It was what I had always been after, this place where God lived, a house of praise.

Something had changed inside of me. Simple as that. A veil had lifted. And I felt the tears of thanksgiving – but there was more.

He wasn't finished yet.

Intuitively, I got the sense that there was somebody else in that room, a fifth party, an invisible presence. It could've been a spook or something, but then things got really weird. As the team prophesied over me, that feeling grew into surety. Every internal question I came up with was immediately answered by the people praying, though there was no way they could have known what I was thinking.

This went on for a good ten to fifteen minutes.

I could feel Him listening, patiently answering. It was a dialogue for two, using four voices. "Your words will be the light for many," they all said, in one way or another. Of course, me being the potentially humble servant that I, by nature, am, my mind ran to Shakespearean power, to lavish gifts, to houses in the south of France, to tall, thin women, Lamborghinis.

But that voice, patient, would bring me back, time and time again. "Your words for the Word, the lesser for the greater, the child for the Man."

It continued, almost wearying me along those sunny beaches.

One of them even mentioned my mother's name, Aunt Amelia's, though I'd never mentioned either to anyone. They recited my room number at the Prince Albert Hotel, named the address and street it was on. He was there all the time: showing me those worn tiles, the Greyhound station, even the TV's, supplying the quarters.

They mentioned third grade, the teacher who loved me.

"I have always been with you," He said. "You are my heart. . . . Come, let us walk together. Things are just beginning for you. . . . Open up in generosity. We have books to read, to write; you have places to visit, people to learn from!"

In the words of those times, the experience blew me away.

What could I feel but gratitude? He had brought life to me with the snap of His fingers, had changed me from the inside out—something that has always remained with me, through the forty-some years which have followed.

It was like summer sea water off Halifax Bay, sparkling on a sunny green beach, cuffs of white water and the belly in sails. Just the breezes blowing their pleasant sway through shoreline trees, leafing high above me, through me, me not knowing where they had come from or where they were going.

Why hadn't anyone ever told me this was possible? Could it have been that the nuns of my youth, though I did love them, didn't know? How could they live a Catholic life and not know this about Jesus, about how He can come?

Having recently read Carlos Eire's *Reformations*, I sometimes wonder what kind of Mass medieval priests were saying. Zwingli, Luther (both had been priests), and Calvin all wanted the same things: no mass — "no mas"; they also wanted more Jesus and more Scripture.

That's crazy. Imagine suggesting to these Catholic Canadian folks that they needed a service that delivered more of Jesus than the Eucharist does! Impossible. Absurd. It was and is literally Jesus, God, the Second Person of the Blessed Trinity: God-food for all of us! And what service could deliver more scripture than at Mass: three readings and all the prayers, each drawing liberally from the Bible.

Protestants don't share nearly as much scripture in their services.

I'm not putting anybody down. As they say, I'm just saying.

Protestants still exist because Jesus needs them.

That's the way I feel anyway. They still point to Jesus in a way that Catholics and Orthodox Christians seldom do. Catholics are always gassing on about liturgy and the good, the true, the beautiful. Tell me about Jesus.

Jesus! That's the Dude's name.

Contemporary Christian poets seem especially reticent.

One hopes they're not trying to serve two masters.

All of us should be forced to wear six-foot humility masks, to ring a bell before us when we walk and talk, especially when we talk about the faith — because, though mostly good at heart, we all carry the plague of self-regard.

After the required hugs, mutual tears, one of the team asked me if I wanted the gift of tongues as well. "Is the Pope Catholic?" I asked, smiling, not a few tears running down my cheeks. The praying again began in earnest, but again, it would take longer than I could manage. They encouraged me to start babbling, incoherently, to allow the Spirit room to take over, and I did so for a while, but it didn't help. I would just start listening to the sounds I was making, putting my attention on exactly the wrong thing. My mind, as ever, was still on me.

The best way for me to beat that, I finally decided, was to imitate the sounds they were making, to concentrate on that, to forget myself as I did so. That way I could give the Spirit some space if He wished.

After ten seconds or so of that, it worked!

New words began to come out, not mine. (This was important for me since I love words, sounds, what they can do.) Each of these new ones took on a new shape, a peculiar size. I felt myself mouthing uncomfortable clumps of blends, vowel units; unwieldy mouthfuls of syllabic groups. Each felt odd, edged, coming out. They made new demands on my oral cavity. But there was an order to each expression as well. I could feel that. It was a tongue of some sort; its sounds delighted me, ones that I had never heard before – ones that I would never hear again.

I was shocked.

God, working in my body! When I said, "Praise You, Jesus," this time, I meant it, even though it still sounded odd. Thanking a man who was God at the same time.

(This would never sell in the fashion district!)

On the way back, I met Greg coming up the wide chapel path. I was pretty animated, gave him a high five, the sound echoing through the dark trees. "Well, what about it?" he wanted to know, his teeth, gritting a little in anticipation.

Getting behind him, I rubbed up the area between his shoulders and neck, gave him the trainer-in-the-corner pep talk. "Lead with the left, the left!"

It was about teatime when I got back. I had to work to contain myself. I saw Suzanne and went over to talk with her, hoping that would anchor me. We had just been discussing this

Life in the Spirit stuff when Ekaterina, who had been walking around the room (I hadn't noticed), came by.

She sat down slowly at the head of our table, as her age demanded, smiled at me.

"So, you're ready to change the world now, hey Honeymooner? Well, that's good. You have a good face. You are on your way. The question is, can you do the laundry?"

"One foot in front of the other," I said, "eh?" waxing Canadian.

She smiled. (I think she liked me.) "Very good. But now you must climb the cross. . . . Don't worry. You will have the words."

Then she turned to Suzanne.

She began, after a short preamble, to talk about her marriage to Fr. Eddie. The two of them had lived the last fifteen years of their lives together as celibates in the community to avoid scandal. "He said it was such a little thing to give up." They both smiled. (I found out later that Suzanne had gotten an annulment before coming up north, was suffering from withdrawal.)

"You can drown in that water," the foundress told her. "This Christian business is no place for the timid. Jesus only asks because you have it to give," she said. "And speak to this excited one," she said, nodding in my direction, giving me a playful shake with her cane. "He may need to make the connection one of these days.'

I had no idea what she was talking about.

Watching her walk away, relying too much on that cane, she seemed a saint to me. (She has been declared a Servant of God—so maybe in 500 years the Church will catch up to her, both of them limping.)

Later that night I wrote a (nearly) successful poem about the Scourging at the Pillar.

6

I don't think I became immediately unpleasant. But it happens to most Christians, doesn't it? The rise, the inflation. It would take its time (and mine), as it does everyone's, gradually at first. Then – and now. I still find myself doing it, speaking a little off-key in conversation, an extra trace of ego, especially if the talk has anything to do with spiritual things.

Back then was my first taste; I began (surprise) to overestimate just how much my conversion had changed me.

I got Periwinkle's first missive that Tuesday after Pentecost. It was nice to hear from her. Her spryness, the spring in her pagan step. Witty, yet seemingly unconcerned, unaware of her spiritual gaffs. She wondered what the fourth-best editor she had ever known was up to in Canada. Would I become a priest? Had they gotten to me yet?

She had moved out, in with George, found a nice little place in Bedford. They were living happily together, "in sin," she said, trying to make a joke. She had taken up painting again as well, she said, always a good sign for her. The quarterly had been out for a while, had gotten bad reviews. It seems the two of them had requested a salary for her like the one given to the University's student newspaper editor. Rebuffed, since literature demanded, in the administrator's estimation, so much less, she and her beau retaliated by printing the rejection letter on the last page of the journal, complete with cloven-footed pig drawn underneath, an "Oink, oink" balloon above his head.

People laughing at their own destruction: the hooves, just as I had done. Obviously, she continued, they were not going to edit the thing next year. In fact, they were contemplating moving to Texas soon, to continue their education in Austin.

I didn't want to hear all this. My past life was a bridge crossed as far as I was concerned. Too much of it was still too close. But how could I keep myself clear? How could I count on being faithful to the new creature I had become, ignore her for starters? That didn't make sense. I couldn't live with my head in the sand.

(Wait!)

I had to stand up, try to speak the truth, belong to what I saw of that. But I couldn't count on the fact that I could keep myself holy by just insisting that it were so. But I didn't want to flirt with disaster either. I'd have to talk to Fr. Pelton about it.

"Old things are passed away," is how I began my slightly inflated response. I told Periwinkle about my Baptism in the Holy Spirit, about everything that had happened, told her that I wanted to shake whatever remained of that selfish life. I didn't dislike her or condemn her, and told her that I hoped for continued friendship. I just needed time to settle into my new life, to digest all that had happened.

Wanting to end the letter on a good note, I said, "God grant you peace. May you know His great gifts: love and mercy, in the times you are sure to face. Look for me when you need me. Your friend, James." I knew it sounded a bit grand, but on the other hand, I had no doubt she would pay for what she was doing.

Maybe her outright rebellion was a good thing, a first step, I thought as I mailed the letter. She had always seemed so fragile in past meetings, as if rebellion were somehow beyond her capabilities. God would take care of her in any case. I would keep her in my prayers.

Gradually, I was moved from the farm to garbage collecting detail in the main compound: incinerator detail. The only time I went to the farm now was when there were big jobs to be done – unloading hay trucks or getting wood shavings for the cow parlor. I liked my new job, got to say hey to everybody on both sides of the road, pushing a little two-bicycle-wheeled wagon. "Get your strawberries, tomatoes," I used to call out, to the delight of my customers. I'd say "Praise God" to everything, if I felt like praising or not, just to keep myself charged up.

People appreciated my enthusiasm. And as spring gave way to summer, I settled into my trips across the compound, the craft and bookshops across the street, the old museum, the girls' dorm, the newspaper house. I'd empty their trash cans, baskets, talk any nonsense I could think of. Each person there living his or her simple life.

Yvonne was still on the other side of the street. I found her a bigger bucket, would collect cones from all over, fill the pail which I'd set on her front porch every third day. But, soon enough, the old restlessness began to return. The first "sort" of summer helped exacerbate the situation as it involved more work than I, or most of the other guests, felt comfortable dealing with.

It started one breakfast when the word passed. Even the well-seasoned hunkered down for the siege; you could see it in their postures. I had no idea of what to expect, but judging by appearances, Saigon, Tehran came to mind. And I was not disappointed. The garages behind the orchard that were filled with boxes were only a part of the story. There was an old convent down the road, now abandoned; the place was brimming with second-hand clothing, books, toys, small household items, stacks of mattresses, box springs, you name it.

It seemed like the whole community, now quite large because of the nice weather, descended on that place. Most of the donations were to go to outlying soup kitchens, some to the places mentioned on the sign next to the main house. Some went to the houses of prayer, not much though, as they were more concerned with praying than with obvious acts of charity. Much went to the rural apostolate down the road, and much was used by the community itself.

No one there owned anything. All the clothes they wore, from their wrist watches to their gym shorts—we sometimes

played basketball and volleyball in the elementary school gym –
had come through donations. The shirt off their backs. And if
occasionally some of them proved a little too eager to reprove,
you had to admit that they weren't half-baking it with their
own lives.

Tom, Mick, and I hefted huge barrels of clothing all that
morning, carried mixed and sorted clothes to rooms assigned.
There must have been three hundred boxes, most of them
large. Nick, as ever, was the comedian, advising me to die to
myself when he passed me, loaded down and sinking as I was.

"Thank You, Jesus. May I have another?" I answered several
times, until I got a glance from one of the women running
the show. I was angry at her unspoken reprimand, started
whistling "O Canada," softly every time I passed her. I figured
I could repent come Confession time.

At one point Tom and I dollied a succession of very heavy
boxes over to the book shop, the bindery. I hadn't even known
the place existed. But there was much about the place I learned
only over time: the hay fields, the maple bush, the iconogra-
pher's hut, the garage and adjacent machine shop, the pous-
tinias – little cabins or rooms one could spend a day in, fast on
bread and water, praying to God, seeking community direction.

It was a great little book shop. Old editions were re-bound
there, stacked, mailed out. Seems they had a small business
going, were in touch with antique booksellers throughout
Canada. Earning money that would go to the poor or toward
buying insulation. (I learned there had been quite a hubbub
about that. Should they be one with the poor of the region
and not have any, or should they get some and put it in to save
money, and thus be good stewards? Ekaterina got out-voted,
though apparently, she did have veto power. It was installed.)
No stone was left unturned by these guys. They even reused
their large envelopes, old string.

We hauled boxes until we collapsed on the grass, then got
up and hauled some more. Ekaterina saw me sling a barrel
over my shoulder, encouraged me with, "That's right. Put your

back into it." She was a sensitive woman, if quite out-spoken (I liked that part), and I'm sure she didn't mean to sound like a slave master. She was delighting in my willingness to do God's work. But it began to bother me as we approached the afternoon. I began to think about the outside world. Maybe I should leave soon, get started.

It was quite an operation, though. You had to stand in awe. Women sewing, re-beading blouses, needle and eye under the early summer sun. Women and men guests doing whatever was asked of them. Everybody shuffling boxes, sorting, out on the hot lawn.

Tom set one down, sweat glistening on his furrowed brow. "Man, nobody works this hard in the outside world."

"We should pay 'em by the hour. . . . give 'em the next war, I say."

He said he wished Jean-Michel were still around to enjoy the festivities. He had left the day before, barely leaving a wake in the water, and that was not rare. So many people now, in and out. A quick hug and an address and they were down the road, you after your job for the day. It was kind of sad, actually, people exchanging addresses, most knowing somewhere inside them that they would never make it over to their friend's part of the country. You had to figure how close of a friend you were. Should you offer or not? There was nothing more painful than watching someone collecting information from a reluctant or surprised pal. Everyone was charitable and all, but nobody missed that type of thing. Tom asked me how long I was staying.

"Ah, I don't know. I suppose I should start thinking about my vocation soon enough. What about you? How's your mom?"

"The nuns next door still looking on her, but I've really got to get back soon. It's dead summer now, and work has started to pick up. A friend of mine and I've got a small business going. Inner-city house repair, at reasonable rates. That kind of thing."

"Charity work whether you like it or not." He smiled, shook his head in assent.

"Are you going to look up your family in Denver? If you go that route, I've got a buddy out there who could always use a good hand. Construction work. The money's good. I'll give you his address and phone number before I go. I'll write him just in case you decide." I thanked him, said I might take him up on it.

Then it was back to the mines.

By afternoon tea, things had slowed down, at least for us. The women were still busy as bees, tireless. I thought about vocation. What would it be like to be a priest? I had to admit, I was kind of a pulpit guy.

"Well, it's something to think about," Father said, puffing on his pipe. "Naturally, I would recommend it." We both smiled. He was a good-looking guy, from Yale, could have married, been very successful if he'd wanted to.

"It's a special calling, to be an instrument. To become clear, not a speck of dust." Here he got quiet, a little inward. But then he picked up. "And then of course, there's the Eucharist," he said, laughing, spreading his arms open wide, getting up from his chair, conveying clearly how much it meant.

In many ways this community life was all I could've asked for. It had the earmarks of vocation. It offered prayer, challenge: intense personal work, consolation, a chance to really be there for people. And there was always something going on.

That weekend, for example, someone had set up a volleyball net in the large space between the sheds and St. Paracletus, in front of the pumps. Staff members, Jim and Patrick, a few priests, visiting and regular, male and female guests, all of us engaging in good sport. The laughs, the banter, the poor unfortunate who, always on such occasions, tends to dominate because of his skill, trying delicately to assert himself.

You can always see the burden on their faces. Moving people around in the nicest possible way, the quiet looks, almost unnoticed when someone messes up. To the priests' credit, they knew just when it was time to call it a day. The fun had peaked, play and attitudes were just beginning to get ragged. Everyone left, sweaty and happy.

Many of us went swimming just to cool off.

Eighty-five degrees, no black flies, and a clear river in front of the house. Greg and I had a leisurely time on some inner-tubes, drifting far out near the center of the river until motorboats and skiers made us retreat. The women had their own swimming locale farther down, across the house. We lamented that we could hardly even see them, decided eventually to pillage the town, eat chocolate.

We stopped at St. Joe's, and Mary Kay invited us into their house, across the lot from the apostolate for a "beverage." (I've never personally used that word.) They offered us some tea, talked to us about the plight of the rural folk around there. Some lived way up in the bush, had no electricity, no plumbing or running water. But they all had TVs. We all laughed.

As I looked out the front window toward the reeds and recesses of the river, Janine answered our questions, spoke a little about herself. She had been a speed skater, had been on the Canadian Olympic team, in fact, but found her life wanting. On current vacations she still pursued her athletic bent, went camping in the National Province Park about a hundred kilometers away, lived on what food she could find there. She'd go white-water rafting with a friend, another staff member.

Even though she was forty of so, she still had an athlete's walk, the slight jerk in it that demanded more of her step than it was inclined to give. She was a nice-looking woman, and I wondered how lonely this kind of life could get.

"Loneliness is part of the package, you know. It's part of any vocation. It's Christ on the cross: suffering. Embrace it and you're free. Avoid it and you die anyway. It's either death or death. One brings God glory, the other brings nothing. Not much of a choice, eh?" she laughed.

"You can't avoid it, so it becomes a question of what you do with it."

At this she looked me quickly, deeply in the eyes, as if she were looking for something, as if she were measuring my depth to see how much pain I had endured, how far I had progressed. I averted my eyes, but it was too late. I still live far closer to the surface than any real growth would allow for — felt ashamed, angry.

I was upset, too, in knowing what she'd done, felt summarily dismissed.

For her part, she didn't seem to give the episode a second thought, continued. "There's a slow pain you come to, have to go through every day. You can feel yourself being refined, and because of that, you take all you can take; and then the next morning you begin again, take some more. You slowly become 'a living sacrifice of praise.' And then one day, as Ekaterina says, it's not so much for you anymore. It's for others. The joy is always there.

"I've seen her do it, take on other people's pain. She calls it a joyful crucifixion.... Have you ever seen the Bernini statue of St. Teresa of Avila, the one with her in ecstasy, with the pierced heart? That's what she means, I think. A painful ecstasy. Sometimes the Lord floods her with that joy, and the loneliness seems to die a little. But it's always there, her cross."

"Can't she just pray that away? Why does she have to take on other's pain? Jesus has already done that, hasn't He?" I asked.

"Then who benefits?"

"What about my life, don't I get one too?" Greg asked.

"So what if you're obliterated?" she asked, looking at us smiling. "Whose will matters here, yours or God's?"

It was too much.

"Some pretty heavy stuff," Greg said outside. "Want to set ourselves on fire tonight? We could be Buddhists or something. Vietnam monks."

We were both too absorbed to talk much, so we grabbed a couple of Canadian candy bars from the General Store, headed back.

I worried. How was I supposed to keep the joy? I couldn't go around reciting the rosary every minute of the day. I discussed that with Fr. Pelton that night and was grateful for his laughter. Don't worry, he told me. Jesus loved me. He wouldn't let me go; then he suggested poustinia.

The one-room cabin was out in the boonies, even for this place. Just beyond the younger male staff's main quarters, a hay field between us. Inside my little home-away-from-home-away-from-home there was a wood burning stove, a thin cot, a table and a chair, a Bible, a four-foot-high red cross hanging on the wall with a crown of thorns looped over it.

I didn't really know what to expect from all of this, messed around a bit with the fire, kindling and paper stacked next to the stove, just the one room, mortar, and thick logs, bounced on the bed for a bit. Taking my time, I read the whole Gospel of St. John, tapped my fingers on the desk after that. Finding a pad and a pencil in the drawer, I took to drawing sunny faces. Got even more restless.

Tried a poem.

I began feeling like a little kid, like I should have had some jacks and a ball to bounce on the floor, though I'd never learned that game. Here I was again, with myself, my boon companion. "Hi, James." "Hi." We got along fine.

I went outside. Felt like taking a long walk, but then I figured that, since I was here, I really should do the tour. I flopped horizontally on the hard bed, said a rosary, and felt, perhaps because of that, a minor expectancy. For what, I couldn't really say, so eventually I let it go, decided to ignore the feeling. Finally, even though it was the middle of the day, I slept.

The sleep itself was uneventful, at least as I remember it, but as I began to come out of it, I saw her – the Queen of Heaven. The most beautiful woman I have ever seen. In white robe, gold trim. She didn't say anything, but she had such a profound sense and look of peace and meekness to her that she didn't have to. She just stood there, praying, not looking directly at me, smiling a hidden, lovely, slight smile of complete faith.

Why she came in this dramatic way, I don't know. I don't even remember if my eyes were opened or closed, or if I were completely awake. I only knew that I was not sleeping.

Maybe she came to show she was, perhaps, that she would always be with me. I don't know.

(As the dung-beetle said. "It was no dream.")

The peaceful effects, fruit, stayed with me in the long twilight, and beyond, as I prayed, more easily this time, washed in the miracle of her ordinariness. I took quiet delight in the good wood of the cabin, the floor, windows, the stars (outside for a breath). There was something wonderfully worthy in the dirt that made up the planet. I squatted down and cupped my hands to hold some. How cool the soil was, as night settled in. I realized how creation answers, always, to the call of life.

I wanted to be like that dirt. I wanted to be there for God's hand, for any seed He had for me. And the grasses. There was great peace in their movement. Why had I been missing that? My heart overflowed with a simple, profound gratitude. This was all God's. He had made it, and it all spoke of Him in some way. Every step along the path. And the path itself, all of it taking me to Him. How could I ever be separated?

And Mary, there, helping at every turn. But I wondered, the more I thought of her: why in white? Whenever I had seen her, in grade school or in churches, she has always been dressed in Lourdes blue.

Eventually, though, it was time for sleep, so I bicycled my legs several times through the cool sheets just to feel the cold give way gradually to warmth, like I used to do as a kid.

The next morning at lauds I was still mulling over the blue and white question when this guy I had never seen before, from outside the community – a very rare thing – brought in a big statue of Mary into the chapel. White, gold piping; he had been carrying it around the world: Our Lady of Fatima. I was amazed. A miracle of coincidence. In my face.

I excitedly told Father Bob on the way to breakfast, but he didn't seem to think it any big deal. (He probably didn't want to encourage me in my visions.) I felt kind of angry that he didn't share my enthusiasm. I needed to be reified in some way, to feel that I mattered.

(Adults were weak. You can't count on them.)

As I began making my rounds with my silly little cart, I wondered what the heck I was still doing in this place anyway. Hadn't I gotten my commission? Wasn't it time for me to go out and meet the world. Sure, a lot of people stayed on and became staff members, but that wasn't for me.

My life in the world had not been a great success, so I felt like that's where I had to go.

I read some Francis de Sales (tough sled), *On the Road* (better).

Nick was taking off the following week, so I talked to him about it and decided that would be a good time to go. I called Tom's buddy to get the go-ahead and then had to live with the anticipation a possible future can generate. The prospects kept me adrenalized, impatient, but I kept a lid on it, went about my duties like a grim storm trooper.

They published my poem in the community newspaper. My first world-wide publication.

Cool. (A Fr. Pelton push didn't hurt.)

7

We stopped at Woodstock, Ontario, to visit some Ukrainian monastery Nick was onto. It was a sad sight in many ways. A few old boys who only spoke Ukrainian and a younger man, about forty, who seemed to have been sentenced there by the Vatican, occupied this huge empty farm. The old guys were holy, though, childlike, cute even, with their big, happy cherry cheeks, glasses. One beamed at me as he offered soup, even though neither one of us understood the other.

The house had three stories and rooms upon rooms to spare, a big chapel as well, too big for the monastery, it seemed to me, with its statues, unused front. Three tabernacles graced that area. There were rows and rows of votive lights, a tall dome above, room for about 150 people, and there they were, five old boys, singing their office in the choir loft. No one on the main church floor. They had a lot of land outside, too, though they had only planted a medium-sized garden. Apparently, they were waiting for the bigger order back east to decide what to do with them.

It seemed absurd, metaphorical. The old church, good, but wasted, going, unused as it was by younger folk who only spoke (what would later become) MTV. Like joyful nincompoops, those old monks stayed there, waiting for people who would surely never come, waiting even past the hope of that. Because they were put there ultimately.

How few come to the obedient voices that can help.

The younger man was a different can of corn. He had tried to make waves, changes, and was sentenced here until the order could figure out with to do with him. Vatican II apparently had charged him up. He was hungry for change, stalked about the place with Nick and me, telling us all about it.

He could have devoured a lion.

We spent a couple of days there, me mostly stewing, and then it was on to the familiar Greyhound station in Cleveland where we split up. Glad hands and addresses. It was good to be back! I started to call Judy before I hopped a bus westward. But when I picked up the phone, I had a change of heart.

I'd pray for her – but why open old wounds? I had a job waiting for me, a new life to start.

A Jack Attack

For when the mark was made *they* saw it.
Nor stopped to reckon the fallible years,
But rejoiced and followed,
And are called wise, who learned that Truth,
When sought and at last seen,
Is never found. It is given.

"Triptych for the Living," William
Everson (Brother Antoninus)

Before heading west to Denver, I decided to touch base with the P. machine, just to see what she was up to before I passed Cleveland through my system. Turned out she and George had gone to Austin as planned, leaving by appearances debris all over the road in their wake.

It wasn't easy, getting her address from her mom, but once I played the Catholic card, I was good. Who knew, maybe I could do a ministry in Denver? I could offer small crucifixes or yarn rosaries to my Beat brothers and sisters! So I zipped off a quick postcard her way, gave her Tom's friend's address in Denver. And then, filled with possibilities, too much of myself, I decided to go full sail. I could hitch across the country rather than bother with the one hundred tiny stops the Greyhound would surely make. I wasn't short on cash, or youth, so I set my sights on crashing under bridges, meeting strange and exotic road people.

Getting out of town, and to the state line for that matter, was mostly a case of stringing short rides, glad metaphorical high fives to my drivers. I tried to beam (softly) along the side of my bag, carry Jesus, look like someone who would be good to talk to. Things went along okay, too, until my only major ride. A '56 Chevy, with a fellow hitcher in the front seat.

The driver gave me a quick wave, never looking back from his steering wheel. He said he was heading to the Springs via Denver, asked me brusquely if I had any money for gas.

"No problem," I said, thought "Thank You, Jesus," for the ride. This was going to be a snap.

"Greetings, brother," said the other, thinner fellow. "Even

if a holy kiss is out of the question, I salute you. My name is Ezekiel, not given, brother, but taken, in the name of the Lord. Have you been saved?"

I looked at the driver as I was handed a tract; he just shrugged his shoulders at me through the mirror.

"Well, yes, as a matter of fact." I thought of Fr. Bob. "That would be a way of putting it."

"Guessing don't get it, brother. Either you washed in the blood or you ain't. Lord ain't got no place at the banquet table for the lukewarm, now," he beamed at me, looking friendly, handing me two more tracts.

"Getting saved won't keep you on board. We're all still sinners. That never changes."

"Terminology ain't mine. Says it all right there in the Book: saved. You got to confess it publicly. Shout it from the rooftops. Got to eat the Word, brother. You can't go round talking fancy talk, trying to sound in-tel-li-gent. . . . Course denominations don't like to hear that. Each one wants to take over, sound real good in the process, smooth and useless as bad butter. Know what I mean? They want to decide for theirselves who get in. But I tell you the Lord is going to wipe the slate clean. Yes, sir. He don't like his voices bottled up. No way.

"No, buddy. Can't get saved in a church. That don't work. The Church ain't buildings. Church is in the heart. Anybody who worships in a church is risking hell fire."

He had cut me off.

I felt offended.

Still, I had to try and love. "But how do you know your theology is correct? There are a thousand Protestant sects. . . . 'May they be one, Father.' You guys are always picking and choosing without any larger sense of context."

"Context, schmontext. It's written in English, ain't it? The Word's all anybody needs. That's all I'm saying. I don't need nobody to 'terpret what's right in front of me. That's for liars and Catholics. Priests. Only fools and hypocrites believe that stuff. You go to church?"

"Catholic," I said.

"Whore of Babylon. Satan's primary weapon. Brother, you've got to get out of there, quick." He kept at it, a pope of one, a church of one, the gleam of rebellious righteousness in his voice.

(I was used to my own version.)

He was past talking to, but that was only one level of the problem because he was like a dentist's drill: loud, unremitting, painful. And he just kept grinding, trying repeatedly to discern if I were among the elect with what he thought were pointed questions. What kind of Baptism had I undergone? Had I been sprinkled or dipped? When did I celebrate the Sabbath, on Saturday or on Sunday? Did I believe in that Trinity business? Did I know Jesus personally, and then, how personally, what did I mean by personally? . . . Had a priest taken part in this praying over process? What kind of Satanic rituals had I been party to? Did I worship Mary, the saints, did I drink holy water, cannibalize? Did I carry pentagrams or relics of any kind?

After fifteen minutes or so of his increasingly inane questions, banter, I asked him to stop, told him he was giving me a headache.

That worked for a few miles, but soon enough he was at it again. First with comments out of the side of his mouth. But eventually he turned my way again, stood up (sort of) and began another barrage.

I rolled down the window, but that didn't help.

(I had to reel my dog head back in.)

Finally, I told him he was a fool, that I sided with William Blake, that his Jesus was my Satan.

Didn't help.

His voice elevated in pitch, and he began to sing-song the book of Revelations at me. (He had a sacrament for every Apocalyptic horn, a Catholic metaphor for every diabolical symbol.) It was too much, and so I decided, somewhere beneath thought, that I wasn't going to give up this ride for this meathead. The driver was going right to Denver.

I started tittering to myself before I did it.

(Such are the noises of the elect!)

I waited for a pause then blasted him with a left hook, hard upside his right ear.

He turned completely my way, stunned as he crumbled up, back toward the dash. He tried to raise up, his voice now beginning to squeak. But I was too fast for him, and before he could figure out how to retaliate, I punched him harder in the nose, blood shooting everywhere as he sprawled back against the door as the car swerved for a moment, laughter coming from the driver's side.

The preacher tried to get up, holding his bleeding nub with his right hand, flailing at me with his left, trying to preach invective as he attempted to beat me off. It didn't help. I slapped him in the face, spun him around by his shirt until he was back in his seat, told him to sit there and shut up.

From above him now, I told him that, yeah, indeed, I was the Munster Inquisition, an angel sent by God Himself to cleanse the earth of all the rebellious who would usurp the authority of the Vicar of Christ.

I called the driver by name, Gabriel, my brother, in a large voice, ordered him to pull over—which he did with obvious glee. Then I jumped out of the car, yanked open the door and grabbed the kicking, cowering prophet by the scruff of his neck with both hands, sent him sprawling among the pigs to forage for the rest of his days (for ten minutes anyway).

He stumbled, tried to stand upright until I took a step toward him. Then he backed away, scooted on the ground.

I got back in the car.

And as we began to slowly drive away, I charitably delivered one last volley. I told him his knapsack would be waiting for him five miles down the road, that I would be waiting for him in his recurring Catholic dreams until he repented and sent chocolates to all the priests in Toledo.

"Great," the driver said shortly thereafter, hitting the steering wheel with the fat of his palm, tears running down his cheeks. "I've been wanting to do that for the last eighty miles. I had visions of listening to that guy through two time zones."

"The 30 years' war in twenty seconds," I said, still rattled and in a huff. "What do ya think?"

The driver nodded toward the glove compartment, said there was an ounce of herb inside. I passed it his way, told him I'd pass. After a few cloudy moments, he asked me why, his voice catching in his throat.

"A, a new leaf . . . almost!"

"Ah, don't worry about it. That guy was a real tool. Must be my lucky day," he responded, shaking his head. "Two of you. . . . Still, I like the way you turn the other cheek, his that is. And the preacher-man is down!"

"His road to heaven," I said, my hand shaking some. (What an ass I was!) Three days out of school and already I was beating people up. What was next, a little grand theft auto?

Confession.

St. Jack, pray for us.

"I'm going all the way to Denver, but I've got to make a few stops. Two aunts of mine. . . . They'll probably feed us."

The more interesting one lived near Danville, Illinois, in a little farming community. She was, surprise, a dyed-in-the-wool Baptist, and I sat with her and her nephew on the darkening front porch, the "holler" as she called it, just behind the house.

"The Lord ain't gonna 'llow much more o' this. No, indeed," she said. "The greed in Washington, everything this country once stood for going down the drain." She rocked back and forth in her favorite chair, riding the first ripples of apocalypse, a cool trace of breeze in the air. Junior sat on the step, me farther back, against the wall of the house, on the tongue and grooves. There was too much immorality, she said. "On TV, in the newspapers. Sin being flaunted at every turn. No, sir. The cup is over-flowing."

Her husband, who showed up later, was a whole different animal. Full of rural mirth, he talked (alone) around their table about some guy down the road who couldn't raise an umbrella. By late that evening he was trying to convince me that someone he knew had a cow who'd escaped his confines by jumping over a six-foot high fence.

I'd seen cows kick in Canada and was shocked by their power and agility, but I didn't want to be played here. So I just sat back, smiled. Like all farmers, he talked about how tough things were getting, and like most of them his ride was a late model Caddy.

I enjoyed them both, wondered where they met in conversation. Maybe his farm moved into her apocalypse; maybe his humor moved them both out again.

The rest of our trip westward proved uneventful, if you don't count the two speeding tickets. (He was in the military and so got out of both.) And then there was the fact that his three on the floor kept slipping out of place through Kansas, eastern Colorado. We had to take turns holding it down for 50-mile increments. He dropped me downtown early, by the city's university, and with an irritated wave (the demands of the car had made us both a little cranky), disappeared down the road and out of my life.

I was hoping for some fireworks: Larimer Street, the old clock tower, My Brother's Bar on 15th, Confluence Park right there as well. The Morey Mercantile Building, Five Points, the whole nine yards.

I thought about Carolyn Cassady as a UD student at the Colburn Hotel, the bar downstairs!

El Chapultepec!

Sonny Lawson's Baseball Field for God's (good) sake.

Denver, baby!

Neal, Kerouac, Ginsburg, Dylan, Waits, Cohen, Mitchell. (Okay, the last four came later.)

"Here comes everybody," as Joyce put it.
Me at least.

2

I felt pretty grubby wandering onto the campus so early, tried to ignore the looks of inquisitive security guards. The U of D didn't have a housing board, but housing books instead, and they were chained to a desk. The worker there demanded proof of registration.

So, I hitched over to Larimer Square, hoped I could find a place to ingratiate myself.

Not five minutes later, this slightly bug-eyed curly headed good-looking guy walked past my bench and duffel, stopped.

"Why you reading that shit?" he asked.

"*The First Third*? . . . I couldn't find yours," I said. "Help me out here."

He shook my hand. "What's your name?" I told him. "Don't worry, I'll get you one. But you won't find any Beat poets worth a shit around here. You must be from out of town. It's all high school kids. . . . Give me some Bergman, Truffaut, a little *Love and Death*, James. The Tattered Cover isn't bad on some nights. . . . But we can do that later. . . . Come on, let's get some breakfast.

"Sheep, James," he said as I got up. "Let's poke them in their eyes with sharp sticks. Whad' d'ya say?"

At that moment he spotted a nice looking, brown-eyed woman walking toward us across the street. "Wetzel, get over here," he said, as if it were an emergency. "Where have you been?" And he immediately smothered her with what looked like a cross between a hug and a wrestling hold, rocking her back and forth, joking all the while about what he was going to do to her.

"James, Philly. My primary reason for living. The loins of my life." She seemed to like his rantings, pulled in close alongside of him, under his arm.

He had a nice intensity about him, as if he didn't care about the small items on the menu.

"Fuck those housing people, James. Do you hear me? Fuck them all. What you need, James, is real help, and, by God, I'm just the guy to do it. . . . There's room in my building. Is this synchronicity or what? Ha ha. God, this is great. . . . Come on, Wetz and I'll show you. It's cheap, easy access. . . . Phil and I are heading in that direction right now, aren't we?"

"Sure," she said, pulling him down to her by the shirt for a moment as we walked, looking him in the eye.

"She wants me, James," he said in an aside, just loudly enough for her to hear.

The guy had his own style, no question, had parlayed a conscious lack of tact, rudeness into a way of life. At least he wasn't a still life. That was good. I didn't want to get up with any more preachers.

"Philly and I are going to engage in some slavering, tie me up with handcuffs morning sex as soon as we get to my place. Isn't that so, my little carnivore?"

"Yeah, but let's not forget my paper."

"Paper," he said with a huff. "I'll give you material for a paper," he said, lifting his one leg up again, trying to twine it around her waist at the same time, rocking her slightly. (It was as if she were struggling against him in some way, though she wasn't.) "Fuck papers, Philly. We have mattresses that will test us." Then backing off, he grabbed her arms as if he were going to subdue her. "I'm tying you up until you scream little screams," he said, proceeding to make little screams. "Oh, Ran, don't . . . stop. Don't stop, don't stop." And then back to his regular voice. "You want me, face it. You can't live without me. . . . help me here, James. I'm losing ground."

"Too much for me."

We seemed to be nearing his place.

"Philly will stop me, after six hours. Won't you, with your mad little whimperings?"

"If I could've, I would have a long time ago, Ran."

The series of apartments were nice, old, the upper floor of a two-story; a coffee shop, sewing shop below. Lots of old trees, a bus stop with old slatted green benches on the boulevard. I couldn't have chosen better myself. I told the landlord I had a job waiting for me.

The rooms were pretty big, bare. Furnished with just an old dusty couch, an older lamp, a TV with legs. It had a tiny kitchen, a stove, a refrigerator, both well worn, but in usable condition. A slightly sweaty-smelling bed, a dresser in the other room.

It beat the Prince Albert in a can.

The landlord was thorough. He showed me waste cans, how to arrange them so the handles were accessible; he showed me the garage, my spot, if I ever got a car; the parts of the building that needed, and would get, work. He told me for a second time that he would get me a new mattress. It took him some time to find his receipt book.

I paid, was in.

There was no answer at Amelia's, so I called Tom's friend, who seemed happy to hear from me. Yes, he still had work, filled me on what they did, what he was looking for. My wage would be ten an hour if I worked out, under the table of course. (At one point he put me on hold for five minutes, had to remedy some small family emergency.)

Tom's word was good enough, he said. I could start next Tuesday.

I got directions, told him that I'd hitch out.

I slowly circled the block, then widened my survey, found a good-sized bookstore. The people were nice, and they allowed me to read in a nice high-winged plush chair for an hour or so. I came away with a local anthology. When I got back, I found

Ran sitting on the concrete steps out front. "Where the hell have you been, James? We can't sit around here all day. . . . there are things to do, changes to consider, and laundromats, James—what about them?"

He took me for a late breakfast to a little diner around the next corner and up the block. Eggs, a huge portion of hash browns, orange juice, coffee, wheat toast, cheap, all beneath hip posters of long-ago western heroes, the latest arty newspaper off the rack. He talked to the waitress, Betty, like they were old pals.

"Betty, this is my friend, James. Jim, where are you from?"

"La Paz."

He laughed. "Betty, this is James from La Paz. . . . He's new in time."

He liked the slip and continued. "Yes, he's knew in time—and in town, and I wanted to show him the kind of service and class this place is noted for. . . . I think we could show him a good time. . . . Come with us after work. We'll go to the art museum. We can cut up the Impressionists with my Swiss Army Knife. I hate the Impressionists, don't you, Betty?"

She was friendly. "Sounds like fun. But, geez guys, I've got macramé class tonight," she said, tapping her pencil against her little ordering pad.

"Oh, I see, Betty. The old macramé line. . . . James, there's a place around the corner where you can wash your clothes for thirty five cents, dry them for a quarter," he whispered, the aside letting her know, perhaps, that he had a real life going on here and that he was really just a generous guy.

(He was.)

"Betty, Betty. Say, how good is that Western Omelet?"

He just kept going.

We ate and talked, she with us for a good deal of the time. He'd stop her in mid-flight, interrupt her with profound questions about art, literature, as she tried to service other customers. He was from Iowa. Son of farmers. It struck me as funny. I couldn't see this guy working the fields.

He said it wasn't so bad nowadays, combine cabins, air-conditioned and sound-proof. Put on some Marley or Clapton and make it happen, James.

He told me he'd been kicked out of the U there for fighting. (My kind of guy.)

He pulled his book of his poems out from the inside pocket of his jacket, flipped it to me.

Cutting Bait.

Log Rolling Press.

"Dog."

"Yeah, none of that Marvin Bell crap, Jim; Donald Justice and the rest of those pansies. You're from South America, James. You know what I mean. Think of Bolivia alone: Bedregal, Zamudio, Casazola. Writers, James, not academic pussies."

He worked third shift as a psych ward nurse.

"Yeah, I know, *One Flew Over the Cuckoo Nest.* . . . Pay's good. What can I say?" He told me he'd been an editor for a newspaper up in the mountains, currently worked three long days a week. "And, no, I can't get any drugs," he said, though I hadn't asked.

We talked about transportation. For me it would be buses and my thumb.

"You do have an out of state license, though, don't you?" he asked.

I nodded in the affirmative.

"Good. We'll get you fixed up soon enough."

And then he surprised me, was kind enough to offer to take me to a great bookstore on Monday afternoon, to help me to load up for the siege. But first, he absolutely insisted, we had to do Leadville! It was my first weekend in town, for Christ (our Lord's) sake.

I liked the dryness of the West, tried to take it all in on the back of his motorcycle as we climbed: the white water running clean in the riverbed along 6. No tangles of trees, roots, to slow the passage; just the ever-assertive rock wherever you looked.

White water in a dry mouth.

Sun was out, though.

Mountains eventually rose on both sides, the Eisenhower Tunnel. (I was surprised it went anywhere!) He turned onto 91, and we were in town before dark. His friend Danny worked the mines. They greeted each other with huge hugs, laughter. Danny, fine bits of grime embedded in his laugh lines, apparently made a lot of money doing what he was doing. Two miles underground.

What did they do during a cave-in, I wondered, run for it?

That got me thinking about work again, watching the two of them carry on, play a game of one-on-one basketball under the lights in the back yard. Work. I've always been against it. Service, discipline.

(I sounded like a grade school principal.)

I hoped I'd be able to see my job through. But to what?

We went to a hopping bar that night.

It wasn't long before I spotted a nice-looking woman down the rail giving me a smile. She looked sweet from the distance. I raised a glass in her direction but got pulled away by Ran and Dan as they physically hauled me into their larger circle. One of the miners had grown up in Canada.

(I later found out that Coloradoans back then didn't like Canadians or Texans. Seems they kept buying up property.)

I jumped right into the verbal fray. My first two beers in two months. The first one scraped the dust, mosquitoes from the back of my throat, added something to my throttle.

The second set my sail.

The long, straight-haired lass I had spotted previously had had some time to think apparently, because when I happened to turn around, there she was: big as life, right in my face, smiling. Blue eyes and smooth earth-woman skin.

No obvious make-up.

"Name's Kelly. You're new around here." She offered me a hand.

"Guilty. Name's Derf, Fred, coming and going. . . No, James. Think I should do something with that, though. . . . Daoud maybe. Percy Bysshe. Something without character. . . . Let me buy you a beer."

We got off to a flying start.

"I work as a miner myself," she said, leaning against the bar. "Nearly everyone up here does. Pay is stupid. Rent is cheap. Good beer and music on the weekends. 'Wassail,' I say." We clinked mugs.

"Sounds like a great gig, but is that what you want to do in the big picture?"

"Ran, that's what I want to be. Where you know him from?"

"You know him, too? Can't a girl get away from that man?" I asked, fluttering ma lashes. "Met him around Larimer Square. How did you get wind of this job, anyway? . . . Forgive me, but I keep thinking of those eastern coal mines: smudged Appalachian faces, crawl-holes, the little lights on top."

She laughed. "We wear lights once in a while, but there's plenty of room. Some big-assed trucks down there, tires twelve-feet high." At that point she took a long pull from her Corona. "Besides, I like being here, great cash. . . . and Colorado, you know? High wind, the mountains, the sun and snow, skiing! . . . Good hiking up here. You should hike the divide."

She had some psilocybin on her, was kind enough to sell me a few dimpled buttons, even as she continued to talk Colorado: Telluride Bluegrass Festival. (They'd just started a film festival as well, going to be big.) She ran it down: the Broncos, Strawberry Days, the Greeley Stampede, Red Rocks, skiing in Steamboat, Aspen. She said what she really wanted to do was to start a lapidary business: semi-precious stones, hammered silver.

I admired her silky brown hair, her lively brown eyes, fine skin — soft and rubbery, rosy brown. I wanted to feel it bounce, just a bit, between my fingers. She had a little up-turned nose, a pretty moon-shaped face. A whole grain cereal kind of person.

Mother Earth, let me swallow you! (I found myself singing to myself) . . . And then I saw it coming — stopped. No, I did not want to lay my body down! . . . Well, I did actually — and that was the problem.

Has always been.

I pulled back, even as we danced, me doing Woody Allen-like hand and finger movements across my face.

She enjoyed the fun, me, it seemed, as we drank heartily. (I incurred both holy buttons, an extreme sort of unction.) She sang all the songs. "Aimee, what you gonna do?" I played some pool, at least until the game itself started to seem weird: a constructed game of nettling angles.

I didn't like concept, found it aggressive.

I wanted the unpredictability of streams, flowing water, life.

Besides, the bar didn't seem like a good place to make real contact with people. We really needed to conduct these rituals outside, stop all traffic, set up round earth-friendly stone tables. One could breathe out there, sit on a bench, belong to the bigger earth, bigger beer.

I didn't really know any of these people, this place.

And I didn't want to become a native.

Slipping out into a friendlier night, I walked away and down old darkening cowboy streets, felt like I was in a Western movie. (I needed a hat.) But the longer I walked, the less connection I began to feel with the constructed world. The houses began to look so temporary. Wooden, they promised more than they could deliver. They sagged against the mountains, the swaying trees, the moon, the older stars.

Our human folly seemed great to me. We pretend we are here for the duration, that we control some of this. We don't. I felt like an apocalypse had to come. All the vanity; every pompous building would have to come down, every lie we tell ourselves about who we are.

We were good at the root of things, yes, but we owned nothing—nothing except our passing.

God did not live in these built things. He had not made them.

I wept for our fighter jet arrogance, for our sins, for mine, for all of us. How far we were from where we should be! How much time did we spend, acting as if He weren't here, controlling everything?

The world was too much with us, late, and yes, soon (very soon).

I had a beer bottle in each of my hands, noticed that and set them, empty, at the bottom of a ravine.

Finally, up a rise, on a crest, I lay on a big rock, looked toward the stars of truth. I took out my rosary and began saying the three mysteries repeatedly, in earnest — for the rest of the mushroom ride. The first attendant course proved lovely: layers of perfectly symmetrical shapes performing in sequence when I closed my eyes, moving colors and wakes and progressions; they woke me up in the joyful music that made me.

I walked happily through a sigh of thigh-high ferns, the syllables of a forest floor, green, with the trickle of a spring that sounded out beneath a flock of high, ancient birds. I saw a physical scene: peaceful western Indian tribes, Cistercians in their midst. Then a different one: medieval ladies, early knights, mounted, leather-clad.

All their lives, in front of them.

I talked with the starry night sky, and it answered, deep-voiced — space dust, shears of secrets. The voice took me through space.... I walked into clear earth water, Lake Mead, up to my neck, felt it give heaven as it moved my body.

After some polyphony, Mother Mary and St. Francis appeared on a medieval road, the latter juggling fruit. (She smiled like the great outdoors.) The three of us walked through Assisi, on one of its neighboring mountains. I met his first friends: happy Ruffino, Leo, the slow and wise. The four of them prayed with me in one of their crammed little twig huts on the side of a rise, looking down over the Umbrian plain.

They gave me their happiness, stuffed it in my pockets.

Mary then gifted me with a shawl, tucked it round my neck; then she tapped me on the cheek.

Next were elephants on an African savanna, where I got to walk next to several lions, my hands on their manes. It felt like a new dispensation.

Jesus did not have to speak there because He was everywhere, in every thing, every sound (kinetic praise). He took me back to Madonna House in Canada where I worked again with Tom and Hubert, picking green beans (some guy seated in a kitchen chair played a banjo at the end of our row).

I prayed with them, for them.

Then, after literally hearing a thick tumble of falling Canadian snow, scruffing flakes, a slow, slight, twirling aerial avalanche out of Combermere's sky, I found myself transported, standing next to a very tall angel who sang in the middle of big city street, Chicago maybe – the cars were from the 30s.

I kept praying my beads.

I walked on heaven's bright streets. St. Joseph offered me a pack of playing cards, Shakespeare leaning over his shoulder, in tilted beret.

"Pick one," he said.

I did.

I met my parents. (How I knew that is another question!)

My long-haired dad gave me a feather, whispered a few things to me, though I do not remember what he said. . . .

Hours later, the back door of Dan's Leadville house was wide open, so I walked in – like one more mountain breeze. The door frame, slanted slightly to one side, seemed a fitting welcome. But I was not greeted by angels.

Pre-dawn's flying pillow caught me on the side of the head.

"Where the hell have you been, you madman? Don't you know there are mountain lions up there?"

"I brought one with me. His name is Tim." I looked behind me, call out. "Tim. . . Tim. He's timid. . . . I think you scared him away."

"Oh, great, tripping are we?"

"Yes, a very excellent mushroom. I must write Kelly a note. God and I were having a serious and prolonged discussion. Your name, incidentally, did come up. Would you like to know what He said?"

"No."

"He said, James Aloysius, that's what He calls me. He likes
my middle name. He said, James Aloysius, I bear the seed that
brings the flower. Love your brother in the noise of his making;
love him in the silence that Love is."

"God said that?"

"Yes, from a long time ago, from the Epipaleolithic. I could
hear His ancient voice invent this place, these walls, the mountains. He sounds like water moving."

Ran yawned, called me a doofus, rolled over for more sleep.

I sat there, nerves jangling in the dark—fed on the morning
when it came, as it slowly made its way into the room. . . . I
liked the pace, time itself.

"Man, where were you last night? We were about ready to
send out the dogs. You and Kelly come to blows or what?"

"No, I liked the bar, her, but the place began to confine. The
mushrooms had things to say to me."

"She wanted you, you twit. Kept asking for you."

"No, she was a nice person, but I'm pretty sure she wanted
someone else."

When we got home in the early afternoon, he followed
through with his earlier suggestion, took my ragged self to a
huge old bookstore, Kay's, even brought along an extra back-
pack. With his help I loaded up for the coming months. *Zen
and the Birds of Appetite, New Seeds of Contemplation, Selected
Poems.* Some of the classics: *The Autobiography of Teresa of Avila,
Dark Night of the Soul, The Story of a Soul, Lui et Moi.* Adjacent
poetry: Ethridge Knight, Edith Sitwell, Hopkins, Akhmatova,
Rumi, Khabir. Ran contributed, tossed a few of his own choices
into my basket: Creeley, *Roots and Branches,* Ashbery, Baraka,
Diving into the Wreck, Memoirs of a Beatnik.

We got together up in his place, read poems, and drank all
his beer. We'd run back and forth, down, up the stairs, reading

our fragments—I forgot this, he forgot that; our heads nodding while Charles Mingus and Miles played in the respective backgrounds.

A Love Supreme.

We sat on the back porch later and blew some blue smoke.

"Let's do a reading together sometime at the Cover. A bottle of Mad Dog between us, what d'ya say?"

"Ok."

"Do a 'shroom if you want. That would be very cool. We'll bust up those yahoos. They'll throw straw down, carry us in a palanquin so we won't disturb Verdi's death-throes."

Speaking of death, Merton was.

On my birthday, 6 years before.

Where were all the Beat Catholics?

I could hitch out to Oakland, find Mary Fabilli. I could set up a tent in her front yard.

Things were live at the Magnus household on Tuesday, business as usual as I was about to find out. The guy was tall, blonde, thoughtful-looking, out-going, slightly prominent teeth, with signs of a prosperity gut beginning to swim out over his belt. He was gathering French drain hoses from the side of his garage, dumping them into the bed of his truck as I turned and thanked my ride.

Mac, I was to learn, was the name he went by. He seemed a little piqued at his mates, the three of them playing basketball in his driveway. He saw me, late, despite the noise, introduced himself with a smile. "I'm still looking for a foreman," he said, ruefully amused at his sorry crew. "If you work out, maybe we'll consider that option. We've got a lot of work. I just need a right hand to keep the troops in line. . . . Hey, let's go!"

"Game point," one of them said. The long-haired guy, about five-ten and skinny, in his bare feet, went up for a jam. He would've made it, too, had it not been for one of the other guys, a slightly wider fellow, who undercut him. It could have turned ugly, but the third, the biggest of the three, grabbed and rescued the former.

They all started laughing.

"Kid, you ass. You go too far," the third guy said.

But Kid didn't care. If no one was going to watch him, he was going to get the winning bucket himself. The barefoot guy came over too late, banged him good, but the ball, already up, bounced around the rim a few times before it settled into the net.

Kid raised his hands high.

"Was there ever a doubt?"

"You could've broken his neck, though, I have to admit, it would look pretty sweet to see his goofy head wobbling around."

They all laughed.

"I knew you'd catch him, Klank. You're such a good guy," sarcasm thickening with Kid's last words.

The original dunker was the first one over to the pick-up. "What's up, boss? Whatever it is it has to be safer than playing round ball with these yahoos."

Mac shook his head.

"Southside, boys. We've got a long way to go and a full day ahead of us. . . . this is James. Let's go." I shook Klank's hand as Mac went back toward the garage to get some more tools. Over his shoulder he told me to check with the warden, that she'd set me up with a time card, but to make it snappy.

I hopped into the bed with Kid and Bob or "Just Dude," as he called himself, Klank in the front seat.

"Was this a battle of nicknames?" I asked.

"Sure, man, choose one," Bob said.

"Quick," said Kid.

"Hans, Maimer of Cuttlefish."

"He's going to need some time to think this through," Bob Dude threw in, laughing. "Hey, look at that one," he said, motioning to a girl down the street, adding, "I'd split her in half."

The guy had coke written all over him. Skinny, live, without the self-consciousness of a speed freak. A kind of Dead Head hipness. Kid, however, was different: lots of acid, no doubt. I asked what was the scoop with blood basketball.

"Tension, tension's the name of the game in this world. Anything worthwhile comes out of tension. Thesis, antithesis, synthesis. Hegel was right there. Do you play?"

"Not really."

"Comfort zone. You're blocking. Play anyway. We'll kick your ass for a while. That's how you learn," he and Bob Dude, both laughing.

Bob, I learned, had come west from Springfield, Illinois, to avoid the gens d'armes (drug-related). He was a good worker, except when the Grateful Dead were anywhere within a four-state radius.

"So are you guys Christians or what?" I asked, trying to undercut the seriousness of the question with a half-comic tone.

"Born again," Bob said. "Happens every weekend with me, until the coke runs out."

"Which Christ are you taking about? The historical one or the Cadillac one . . . the One who helps us find the cocaine," Kid asked. They both liked that one, slapped hands.

Kid's face was drawn up tight, tense, in lines. And it stayed like that a good deal of the time. As I looked at him that first week, I began to wonder if he had chosen Hegel because of the tension he was already feeling, maybe using the philosopher to try and turn his self-doubt into money.

"What's real? I think that's the question," Kid answered, handing me a joint he'd just lit. "Try this stuff." And then, to redirect any serious line of inquiry, he comically added, "What do you think of the mountains? Aren't they beautiful?"

Mac did work for an insurance company and business was booming, largely because the builders were such money-grubbers. They'd built long units on expanding soil, could have secured things had they taken a bit more time, built in some real support. But that would have involved long-term thinking. Unamerican. It was our task to right their wrongs, to provide drainage, to drill, install rebar and concrete pillars underground. It was hard work, but fun. We could bust each other all day.

At lunch, we'd usually go to Super's for sandwiches, Cokes, eat in the back of the truck, either that or at a Mexican restaurant if Mac was feeling generous. He usually ate up front with the door and window open in the parking lot. Kid and Klank occasionally would get on me in the back of the truck, razz me about the nowhere my life was going. Was I going to be doing this when I was fifty?"

"Why not? It's honest labor."

"Not the way you do it," Bob Dude said.

"Maybe you should think about a ministry? Gonorrhea victims," Kid said, ending with a tiny stoned voice that conveyed his obviously expressed concern.

"Yeah, you ain't getting any anyway. That's why all you guys turn to religion, ain't it? Hey, wait a minute, none of you are for that matter. Hey, what am I doing here, hanging with a bunch of Alices? Maybe you should all be ministers," Bob said. And then, after a pause, he added, "Klank is waiting for marriage, and Kid. . . no woman in her right mind would talk to Kid." Me and Klank laughed.

Kid always looked on the edge of a precipice. He was proud of the fact that he harassed the weak-kneed at his college, Regis. Get tough or leave was his motto.

"Hear the crackle, Bob Dude. The sound of your butt being fried on the ever-lasting barbecue pit. Laugh now or forever hold your piece," I said, emphasizing the last word. " . . . Any of you guys read poetry?"

"What kind?" Klank asked.

"Beat."

"What, that shit?" Klank asked. "Professional outsiders, huffing their own farts. I'm so real," he said in a higher-pitched voice. "Find me some young boys."

"What about Merton, or your Jebbie, Berrigan?"

"What? . . ."

"Not, really," Kid replied thoughtfully, answering my original question. "Hey, Bob Dude, did the coke come in yet?"

"Holy shit, would you like a loudspeaker or something?"

"You guys are both crazy," Klank said. "They'll be calling your skinny asses Judy in jail."

"Not me, man," Bob said. "I'll be getting them the coke."

"You're both pathetic," Klank continued. "You live for that shit. Why don't you get a life? Are you just going to be chasing the spoon for the rest of your lives?"

"Hey, man, I ain't no college boy. Ya got ta do what you can. It's the American way. Private enterprise."

"Klank wants the middle class: a wife, maybe a fence, a Snapper mower," Kid said, lighting up a joint, cracking everyone up. "Give me Morrison, break down the doors of perception," he said as he took another toke.

"Right here in the parking lot. Kid, you got balls. . . . I'll tell you who wants the middle class life, upper that is. Myrt. That's who."

Kid sank a bit.

"Low blow."

"Blake that was. . . . And hey, this isn't such a bad job," I said, almost thoughtfully.

"God, you're fucked up," Kid said.

At five, we, dirty and sweaty, returned a dump truck Magnus had rented, decided on ambrosia.

"Thank You, Jesus," I said.

"Amen," Bob Dude intoned.

We had a little bit more than we should have at the first stop, and Mac, wanting to appear the generous guy he was, suggested we go to one more place.

It was a topless bar.

The others began to walk in, but I didn't need that. So I pulled him aside, told him I'd hitch home.

"James, you have scruples!" He smiled, looking at the others. "Well, how about that, guys, scruples!"

I had my nickname.

3

Later that evening, I tried to call Amelia again from the phone booth just outside our building. The number had been disconnected. I felt confused, didn't notice Ran's face against the outside glass of the booth for a while. He screamed, jumping higher than I did when I finally made eye contact. As I opened the booth door, I immediately found myself subjected to the indignity of a headlock, him telling me how good it was to see me.

When things calmed, he introduced me to his new girl, Jaime, a slight, curly-haired woman who was standing right behind him. "A nice Jewish girl, James, you wild man. Her mother wants her to be a lawyer. Can you believe that? How cliché."

"I don't know, Ran. Maybe I should buy a Harley, drink exotic coffees. Would that make it all better?" she asked.

I liked her. She seemed on to him.

"She's a poet, James. . . . Don't tell her I admire her, okay?" he said softly to me.

"Ran just wants to be accepted," I added.

She smiled, shook my hand, and invited me to come with them to the corner deli. I was up for it, but was feeling distant, too. They picked up on that, wanted to help.

Where did she live?

"Come on," Jaime said. And we hopped in her car.

There was a for sale sign on the grass, no answer at the door. I walked around, tried to look inside the dark windows.

"Maybe she got evicted, if she was your relative," Ran offered.

Just then a little woman in her 60s, in curlers, came from next door, pulling her robe tightly around herself as she addressed us.

"Are you folks looking for someone?"

"Oh, you must be James. I thought you were at that Catholic farm. Come on inside." We followed her back to her house, where she put on a pot of tea. After taking off her glasses, rubbing them clean, she continued. "I'm sorry to be the one to tell you, but Amelia passed a few weeks ago. . . . A lovely woman, a dear neighbor and friend.

"It was a beautiful funeral, over at St. Monica's."

She suggested I go talk to Fr. John, asked for my address — papers, that sort of thing.

Amelia sounded as sweet as I remembered.

And since I wanted to stay with that vibe, I told my friends I'd catch them back home. I wanted to walk back.

The long stroll did me a lot of good, so much so that on the succeeding nights I did the same thing, just to think about my life. On one of my treks, under the generous, high trees, all the breeze in a Denver night, things took a surprisingly good turn. As I enjoyed the quietly chatting people in their squeaking chairs, the front porches of nice old Victorian houses, one family playing what they could see of croquet on their front lawn, I spotted a woman, three houses ahead. She was sitting by herself on the porch steps of a small ranch-style house, her old German Shepherd, the slight hitch in its get-along, chasing the ball on the front lawn.

As I reached her sidewalk, the dog came right over to me, sniffing the grass at first, as if he weren't really interested. I backed up a step, but he grew friendly almost immediately, wagging his tail, dipping on his front legs, rear end up. He backed up a bit, barked. He wanted to play, and, before I knew it, I was patting his head, scratching his stomach as he flopped over on his back, wriggling around like a snake, making snorting sounds, his nose upside down in the grass.

"Quite a watch dog you've got here," I offered.

"Yeah, watch it or he'll lick your ears off," she said, smiling from her front porch. She seemed friendly in the night, clear as it was, starry as I looked up, the pleasant shake of the towering branches.

"They're a good breed, though. Loyal, strong . . . and playful, aren't you?"

Another bark.

"Nice traits in anyone."

"Indeed." I looked up again. "Beautiful night, wouldn't you say? What kind of trees are these?"

Celibacy is easiest if you're not seeing anyone. I've tried, often concertedly, to do things the obedient way. Usually I've failed, though, especially if the woman in question offered some kind of lived comfort, a sense of tomorrow. Not in terms of commitment, but rather, in the sense that she actually had one.

4

Margaret and I had good times, though she didn't care much about poetry. She would never talk much about what she believed. All she asked was that I not give her any of that hard-shell Baptist hoo-ey. We enjoyed each other's company: good humor, a good movies, some wine. Just the two of us on her couch and most of the lights off, talking, and, in time, I moved closer. Shadows would pass on the walls with the cars, over the antique photos and frames she had managed to collect and hang throughout the years. Some Glen Miller on the radio. It seemed odd to me that all the photos were of strangers. She didn't care about that, though. They seemed to offer a sense of the past, and apparently it didn't matter whose. It struck me then that maybe stability was what she sought, too, some sense of connectedness.

Her sense of self, community, was different from mine. It was larger. She valued the virtue that can be found there, would never place herself above others. They gave her meaning in some way.

I lived more isolated, reticent. I was satisfied with less. Maybe that's the result of some sort of early physical abuse. I don't know.

("I couldn't feel, so I learned how to touch.")

I suppose that is why I've never belonged anywhere.

Even now, as far as my faith walk goes, I don't trust consensus. Over the years, it's usually a pretty good sign that something is afoot. Think of the liberal seminaries and parishes in the 80s – before EWTN: "The Vatican must reassess its position on homosexuality and birth control." (Did that lead to the sex abuse scandal? Would be hard to argue against that proposition.) More recent conservative craziness has come from the other end, from ardent Latin Massers and virtual-livers – idolaters of the good, beautiful, and true: "holy" people who would protect the Church from contaminants. (I actually met a fortress couple who once took the time to assess presiding priests at Mass by how high they held up the Host during the consecration. They'd report all transgressors to the local Bishop.)

Speaking just for myself, I needed then what I need now, to find my meaning in the open air, among people met and mostly passed.

I enjoyed Margaret's company, her peculiar brand of disconnectedness. I was seeking (momentary) resolutions, too, in my way – in the other. Maybe we all do that each time we talk to someone new. In any case, it felt good and comfortable to be there, to spend time with her.

She was worth the effort.

We had our failings.

I think of the "aubade": poetic partings in the post-coital morning; those times when you have to ignore the dopamine, the oxytocin receptors; those strained moments when you can actually feel the delicate gauze of your psyche begin to tear as you leave, open her front door – as you find yourself outside on her porch, a few birds up and singing, you starting to walk down the steps. You cut yourself off from the unity you were made for because the two of you are not yet one.

It's during those rips, minutes, when we can best feel how delicately, marvelously, we are made. All of us, convicted, have to ignore that deeper ingrained, integrated sense of self in order to get on with our separate days. We have to forget what endures.

But what was done, was done, wasn't it? And then, upon occasion, done again. Though our lives, mine and Margaret's, did gather, like flowers, into a sweet bunch once in a while, there was that pull in the other (separating) direction. She had her fears, most unspoken—but who doesn't suffer from that? The goodness of her life was palpable. She had sense enough to seek others, wouldn't allow herself too much time alone. Wisdom there. She'd help out during marathons, get water for the runners; she'd go down and answer phones for the suicide hotline.

For my part, I chafed in her small rooms—maybe because I relied too much on feelings. The square feet of her life seemed to hem me in in some way. Her world began to confine; it felt like a globe which only offered three continents.

It's not that my world was healthier.

It wasn't.

It was less so, but I needed possibility, horizons, too. I had to have that. I needed something to open up into—should that eventuality ever arise!

Another way to say it is that I needed art. I needed a life alive to possibility, to the new, to the loose electrons which fly all about us. She was smart and big fun, but both my healthy needs and my neuroses—who can pull those apart—began to close in.

Sometimes I liked the walls of her beautiful little house, sometimes I didn't.

Had I moved in, I surely would have eventually started writing on them.

It's a hard truth to accept: the Church's teachings on sex and marriage.

Picasso said that genius is 99% personality. You can certainly see that in Dickinson, Yeats, Frost, Stevens. Not as much in the sheriff, Ezra Pound (a very good poet), though on the surface he might seem to be the one most endowed. He had the walk, the plume, the hat, he had flare. But he wasn't. His partner in crime, T. S. Eliot, a crab-scuttling tight-suited neurotic, combed up for his fiduciary shtick, offered a better cafe table in French rain than Pound ever could. The greatest artistic shaker and mover in the twentieth century, though gifted, comes up a little short on the personality meter.

That's art though.

We all hope for a place among the best.

We all find it.

I've always needed possibility like a fix. If the present had absolutely no chance of opening up into something outrageous, what did I have?

In any case, I eventually started to snip, get unpleasant around the corners.

To her credit, she didn't sit still for that.

The strength of her response took me aback at first, and so I quieted, settled back into my place. At least for a time. But that hemmed-in feeling kept coming back. It often felt like my days were literally being knit around me, and I hated the sound of busy grandma needles.

Although I was a little younger than she, actually the gap was larger. In some ways I was still an adolescent – or less. Still am (infantile even). I need a kite, a roomy life, one that doesn't fit.

I can't settle for fit. I had to find my unfinishable life, not settle into someone else's.

Around that time, I got a nice letter from Periwinkle, through Magnus. She and George were still together. Come on down and visit, she urged.

Work soon began to slow at the (construction) health spa, since it was winter by then. so I thought about it. I'd saved up a bunch of dough. Margaret, who made dental molds for a living, and I did cheap things: episodes of *M*A*S*H*, foreign movies in alternative venues, good cheap restaurants, so I figured, "What the heck?" I might as well take a week off, head south, visit my old friends.

Margaret was not new to any of this. She'd been through the wars.

She didn't mind. She said she'd taken a more detached look about us of late, had decided to let go and see where we went. She still seemed to enjoy the good times we had, the occasional carnal embrace, but, at the same time, she wasn't hesitant in asking me to leave if I got on a jag.

I respected her for that, wondered why I didn't love the woman more than I did—wondered why I needed to leave for a time.

"Because you're a wild ass of a man," she said. "Work out what you need to. You've got my number. Call me if you get into trouble."

With that, she kissed me, tapped me slightly on the cheek as she turned up my coat collar before I left.

"Come back."

I had done this.

5

I felt a little confused, empty, full of the appropriate self-loathing. On the other hand, maybe she was right; maybe the space would do us both good. I got together what I needed: Kid's over-hauled truck, some clothes, and hit the open road late one evening.

One more weary-assed time.

(Though this didn't really count as Kerouac or Cassaday's "road" – because I wasn't going to Mexico.)

I couldn't really compare the two situations because all the Catholic Beats I knew about were in jail (Berrigan), or dead, either in Auckland (Baxter) or Thailand (Merton), or had left the friary (Everson).

Once out of Denver, my spirits rose, kicked in with the country western station. I had forgotten how good it felt to be alone, just me and the lined pavement, the sound of that asphalt testing the tires, out on the lone prair-ieee.

I yelled a few times out the window, stopped along the border of some little no-town, Colorado City, turned off my lights, just to watch people drift in and out of their lives, walking streets, going to Denny's, everybody looking for happiness.

(The carrot of God!)

It was an exciting prospect, going to see old friends. I didn't have much to report personally, of course. Just that I was still alive, taking air. When I stopped the truck a second time, just outside of Clayton, NM, I ran after and collected a tumbleweed, gathered two others, flattened against a fence. I put them in the bed of the truck and then went back after the miles, swerving on the empty road into morning.

I called Periwinkle early in the a.m. as I crossed into Amarillo, the mid-point, felt the truly foreign land of Texas. The P. machine did not share my phoned enthusiasm, however, as she had just asked George to hit the bricks.

Come on in anyway, she said; she'd call off at work.

Austin was a nice place, driving in. More trees than was meet perhaps, but, hey, was that possible? The highway ran through the town below street level so the good residents could enjoy their early morning coffee, their paper, the scuffling sound of children's pj'ed feet throughout the house without being reminded of the passing world.

I don't know why I was so psyched to meet her, but I was.

She'd always been fun to be around. That simple, I guessed. There was an innocence to her. And more, she liked me, though not in a sexual sort of way. Platonic – though who knew what possibilities could lurk? But maybe that was just my own energy.

She greeted me at the door with the remains of a cup of coffee in her hand, a smile, the last traces of sleep in her eye. She perked up almost immediately. "Oh, James is here," she said, happier than one could expect in the morning. "Crush him. Crush him," she said, putting down the cup and bouncing up and down as she gave me a big hug, spun me around a couple of times.

"You look good," she said, tousling my hair. "There is much to do. How long are you in for?"

"Twenty to life. No, just kidding. A few days. Don't want to over-stay."

"Great. As long as you like. How are things?" she asked, sitting down next to me on the couch.

"Eh."

"I know that one, but, hey, I called off today, and tomorrow won't be a problem either. We can have some fun. But I do have to go back to work on Monday, okay?"

"So what happened with George?"

"Oh, long story. You know how it goes: boy meets girl, boy retreats girl, duck calls and innuendos. Moose down Main Street."

She didn't want to talk about it; seemed to be doing okay though.

We had fun preparing a late breakfast: tacos, enchiladas, some eggs, potatoes. I chopped the green onions, all the little heads, as she flipped torn lettuce leaves skyward, mouthing their discontent.

She smiled, opened the window behind her, let some air in before we sat down. "There, that's better. Listen. . . . Northern mockingbirds: kind of ironic. But they're great mimics. . . . Look at that guy's tail! . . . There's one who comes around, sounds just like a cat!"

Pure Periwinkle, enjoying the present, more than anyone I've ever known who wasn't delayed. And she was right, of course. When birds were singing in the morning, what else was there, really?

I grabbed a shower and a cot nap. She'd set one up in her front room. I didn't wake up until I heard her keys in the front door. Bags of groceries. She looked vexed.

"What is it?"

"Beer. Darn."

"Wait for me," I said, putting my shoes on. "I'll go with you."

The first thing I noticed were the drive-in liquor gas stations. Pick up some Lone Star with ethyl, a nice couple. "An encouraging sign of the enlightenment, selling beer at a gas station. They should have the jail on the other wing, save everybody time and money."

"Welcome to the best danged state in the Union."

I watched her a bit. High strung. It was probably the little things that gave her the most trouble.

She gave me an apple, bit into her own. Next stop, a Japanese zen gardens just outside of town. It was, like most of her ideas, a good one. There was a peaceful quality to this small-leafed, manicured place. Cool quiet ponds with big orange goldfish who would come up whenever you clapped; the attendant small healing sounds of running water into the ponds from pipes.

The bushes and trees were of the smallish purposeful variety, close-cut and scrupulously cared for, the limbs never unduly cluttered, except where most useful, at the ends. Purple, next to green, seemed the dominant color. There was a sense of aesthetic movement, interconnectedness among the wood, foliage, rocks and stone, fish, the planned structure shaping reality.

And who could argue? Life was best when you felt context, a kind order.

It was unusual to see all that in Texas though, I must admit. This careful and attentive use of space. Did the architects have any sense of the irony, or were they more concerned with teaching their small reality?

There was nothing there drawing attention to itself. Everything spoke the unhurried language of Japanese restraint, the small step, the porcelain face, the kimono, long hair pins. We both breathed it in, walked a little slower on its sculpted paths, felt the good, maybe because a similar place in us had been reaffirmed or awakened.

That night we hit a bar that also ran plays in another section of a massive first floor.

We walked through Capital City. She told me that the state building was one foot smaller than the DC version. Pure Texas. There was a nice park there as well, some Brother Christophers brown bagging it in the cool winter air, a few other couples out for a walk.

She told me she didn't know what was up with her life yet, that this was a good time for her in that respect. George – in a weird way – helped her to see the issue more clearly. And then she wanted to know what was I doing with mine.

Was I going to be a priest?

I wanted to be a poet, though I had no idea how I was going to support myself.

"I wish I had your faith. All I know if that I've got to make a move pretty soon."

We walked across a field of tall grass.

I admired her, her airy personality.

We weren't fifteen feet in when she screamed, leaped backwards. In response, a big dog who had apparently settled there for snooze, lifted his sleepy prone head for a moment, gave her a look as if to ask what the problem was. Then he yawned, stretched some with his front paws, and settled back down.

Periwinkle turned red; you could tell even in the dark.

"Can I hide here?" she asked, ducking her face in my armpit.

In a moment, she came back, different.

"You know, it's so typical. My own shadow. I don't much sound like one who is going to take the bull by the horns in her life, do I?"

"It's a small bull."

I stayed awake for a while that night, wondering what she was doing. Said a rosary. Where the heck was I going with my life? Where would I be in twenty years?

Periwinkle woke up the next morning, the sun in her voice.

She burst out of her bedroom, throwing a wing of the curtain over a padded chair, sang Don Giovanni, or what sounded something like that. She bounced around the apartment, lifting shades. Then she proceeded to sit, jump up and down on my prone back. She was wearing a pink "I love cats" t-shirt, pants that didn't match.

She paused, said, hey, she'd been practicing "The Moonlight Sonata." Would I like to hear it?

"Yes," I said, my head deeper in my pillow.

So she did, nicely.

Closed the lid.

"What shall we do today?" she asked. "How's about a nice drive through the country? We can take some lawn chairs, books, find a willow, still waters. We can paint. Let me pack us some food."

And soon we were at it again, cutting cheeses, carrots, celery, apples, Wheat Thins. She grabbed a few books, a thermos of tea, and we were off.

"You reading all these?" I asked.

"Gives me room to range," she said, munching a carrot. "Besides, I'm thinking of going back to, how shall I put this, college."

"Your mother can get some sleep."

"She won't speak to me. Has my brother call to get information."

"You could lie.... Besides, she just loves you, no?"

"Funny way of showing it."

I did several impromptu ballet steps on the spot to try and cheer her up.

We stopped at a Convenient later to get some donuts and chocolate milk (my idea) to counteract the enzymes in all her healthy food. We took to reading poetry to each other from a Norton Modern in that parking lot. She went for Stevens, I for Williams. She loved the curly-cues and frivolity, artifice, philosophy. It was her style, anything for well-ordered fun. For me it was epiphany, seeing straight, delighting in the chaos of the poor, in what was real.

Like Periwinkle, they both liked art: the Armory Show in 1913.

Loaded for bear, we headed out into the surrounding country-side. There was a certain kind of pleasant distance our Platonic friendship allowed us, probably because we were not a threat to each other. I was free to enjoy her company. It was nice not to worry about how I was doing.

She pulled her car over just to watch the sway in the tall grasses. And then, before we could find an ideal spot on the lake, she noticed some heavy clouds off in the distance. We decided we would wait, watch that, windows open, eating our cheeses, thins. The air, predictably, began to cool as we read some more, gabbed.

Finally, the wind got downright cold, and a heavy rain began to roll in. We wound up our windows, watched until they began to fog up, and then we headed home.

The rain picked up even more as we headed to her place. It was getting colder. That night, after a movie, both of us found ourselves coming out of our rooms, moving repeatedly to the single heating register in her house, took turns standing on it. In the morning, ice everywhere. On branches, cars. The whole town was coated in it. It was great fun. We swung on Robert Frost branches, freezing our hands, throwing ice balls, pushing each other around on a trashcan lid.

When we went inside, warmed ourselves with hot chocolate, I talked a little about what was going on with me spiritually. She couldn't relate, couldn't get past grade school nuns, her mother's vise.

Too soon it was time to leave. I cranked up the old truck with a heavy heart (I felt my pain – said in a Bill Clinton voice). I thanked her for a nice vacation, though I agreed with her that the British work "holiday" was a better choice. None of that Puritanical disdain for having left a space at work, for having deserted the never-ending battle to prove one was among the elect.

We'd do it again some time.

The weather had cleared by then, but I knew the storm had not.

I didn't want to blame Margaret for the way I felt. She was where she lived, who she was. She had found a measure of peace, hung on to what she had because, like all of us, that was all she thought there was to get. And though she moved more comfortably in her space than I ever did in mine, still, I needed room to want more.

6

After that end, the rest of my world began to close up as well. Though I got a chance to read several times with Ran (who'd taken to calling me "Jesus Juice") at the Tattered Cover, once in a Big Bird costume – to nice applause – I had to do something about my work situation. Magnus's insurance connection had begun closing its fist. It was late winter by then, and there wouldn't have been a whole lot of work anyway.

Money was not a problem, but what did I want to do in the big picture? That was the question. What kind of job would satisfy me long term? I wasn't sure until I decided to take a cab to a Charismatic Mass one snowy weekend (which was a great experience until testimony time – then it became King of the Mountain). Jesus, have mercy.

It seemed like good work, taxi-driving, and the driver had a lot of good things to say about it. No one telling you what to do all day. The hours were long, but the pay was okay. You could map out your own day, meet all kinds of people, get robbed once in a while just to spice things up. It could get competitive, sure, other drivers ripping you off, stealing your fares. But what job wasn't competitive? He liked the work himself, made it sound worth checking out.

Ran loved my "small start" Ft. Collins idea, but said I needed to go back to night school.

My first chapbook of poems, *Banjo Messiah*, had found a home: his Log Rolling Press people took me on.

He carried on as usual as he prepped his Sportster for my journey.

"Whatever you do, don't do Naropa," he insisted. "That's group mind, a death factory, Iowa City without the glitter."

Better to die in the gutter with a needle poking a vein.

A Fine and Doughty Place

They arrive
By the stone stairway step a day,
While the winged children strive
Against hysteric winds to stay
Flapping vaguely in the tear-wet air
Calling on the spirit of Prophecy to witness their despair.
"Simple Folk," Patrick Kavanagh

Acclaim — what I've hoped for — has not come. In time, though, every human being begins to see that doesn't matter so much. What matters is that He has, and does, mostly in the inner circle of people who make up our lives: in our spouses, neighbors. And so failure takes on a new, more intimate face, ours: when we don't love.

A good job, a career of sorts, has followed, a lovely family.

Jesus is still the center. He still shakes the world, as He did in the New Testament.

We try to follow, mostly by learning how to give up what we can of our inflated sense of self.

"In His will is our peace."

In our last extended stop, that primal push, that sense of achievement begins its fade, and so feels a bit like a denouement — though that cannot be so, because Jesus begins to spring up out of the ashes. As Roethke says, "We learn by going where we have to go."

That will all take us to Periwinkle, but first, taxi-ing begins:

Squiggle, urk, squiggle: the sound of a saxophone found its way through a slightly opened front window, late winter morning, Oak Street, Ft. Collins, CO, USA. The whole thing seemed so college-y: the music, the bicycle, the hand-made rent sign on the front tree, like something out of a high-plains Ozzie and Harriet. So I put down the kick-stand on Ran's motorcycle, warmed up as best I could right there on the sidewalk. A short-ish dude in a lumberjack shirt opened the door. He had dark, deep set, friendly eyes, a slightly pocked face, brown hair parted down the middle, the sax strapped to his neck. His accent was Boston Irish.

Yes, they needed someone – they being he and his girlfriend, Bobbin. His name was Rill (a good friend, now, for decades). I took him up on his offer to come in and sat down as he unhooked and disassembled his sax, carefully putting it into its purple, felt-lined case. I checked out the lay of the land as he did so, liked it: hardwood-easy wood floors, a rug in the center of the room. There was an old couch with an Indian weaving thrown over it, a pillowed rocker: obviously his with its masculine busyness (small side table, books, pens, pipes, an ashtray), a milk crate for a footstool in front of it.

An architect's table was cornered along the back wall, with a radio, more plants, typed papers on it. Klimpt's "A Kiss" on the wall above the sofa, storage chest in front. A grad student's pad, no question. Learned, hungry, frugal.

I watched him as we talked; he measured his words carefully. The volume was soft, the words somehow working against themselves as he spoke. It seemed as if there was a deep, slow burn going on in his lower bituminous regions. You could see that in the way he seemed to hold himself back, down, in the way his sense of self seemed to emphasize the darker tones of his eyebrows, eyes, as if they expressed what was going on inside.

I liked him.

There was an openness to him. (I would later find out that he was an ex-Catholic, running from what he saw as gospel-violent nuns: those stinging little silver worms, wriggling on struck palms.)

"Yeah, Creative Writing, the MA program. Poetry. How about you? What brings you to this fair place?" irony in his voice.

Another poet, I thought to myself. Geez, was there no end?

"Poetry as well, street stuff, though I want to drive taxi. I'm up from Denver. I want to nail it in a smaller town first, give myself a year or two to learn the ropes. Then maybe I'll take on a bigger city."

He looked at me like I was a little crazy, smiled. "It's $175 a month, shared utilities. . . . I didn't know they had a cab company in Ft. Collins."

"Yep," I answered, pulling out four bills. "Two months and a little good faith. Am I in?" I walked over, looked at my room. "This will do nicely."

"It's okay by me, but I'll need to check your references. You're not out on parole or anything, are you?" he asked with a smile.

"Can you get that here?" I asked. "No, I can give you the number for my po-po if you'd like."

He balked for a second.

"Bobbin's in the bedroom. She'll have to approve."

I watched as he walked a delightfully guarded walk, short steps, over to the bedroom door. After some whispering, she came out; young, in bathrobe, pulling her bangs down over her eyes. Her accent, too, Boston.

"Hi," she said, smiling, bright brown eyes, shaking my hand. "I had to work the late shift last night. Want some coffee?"

I followed them into the kitchen, and then all of us, back into the living room for polite (little fingers extended) cups and conversation.

"Rill says you want to be a cab driver. Ambitious, don't you think?" she asked, laughing. "Just kidding." She looked across at him, then back at me. "But I mean, is that it?"

"Can you make a living doing that around here?" (sinuous) Rill asked.

"I want to go after this. It suits me. How much money does one need anyway?"

Rill pulled out a joint, lit it, passed it my way.

"A lot."

"Na, thanks, I'm doing a Catholic thing. . . . Look, I've got to get to the cab company, meet with the boss before the place closes. . . . Here, take this," I said, pulling out a fifth of Jack Daniels, gave it to them. "I'll come tomorrow with my clothes and stuff."

They looked at each, approved in their ways.

They proved quite generous, as friends, editors. Rill took me occasionally to program get-togethers: volleyball games, iced beer, a happy mushroom group trip to a mountain cabin once – all of it delivered in a slightly suburban way. And that was fitting. These guys were after success: either in academia (if you were a poet), or maybe some bank if you wrote fiction. They almost seemed to function as a team. They pulled for each other, would brag about mutual coups.

As for me, I've always wanted the other side: people at spiritual loose-ends, mechanics, those who don't fit in.

The owner, Jim Bells, was at the mike in the office, one in a long row of frontage offices: corrugated roof, cheap stone, stretching perpendicularly off the road. He seemed friendly, smiled, waved me in through the big picture window, all the while talking to an apparently thick-headed driver.

"No, she said she was around the back. The second building to the left. The Durango apartments. Number 6-C. She said she'd be out there looking for you."

"I see building F. There's HH over there. So I must be going in the wrong direction, huh? I don't see any building C, though," came the static-filled reply. "Is there another driveway? . . . Wait, there she is. Must be her, running over now, kind of limping. She's waving at me."

"Good, be nice to her now. You've put her out, being so late. She wants to get to the hospital. It sounded pretty important."

"Ten and four. Over and out," came the slow reply.

"Drivers," he said to me, stretching back in the chair. "You just can't tell what you're going to get."

"How about me?" I asked, smiling, pushing the hair on my head off to the side, trying to look cab-like. "Sharp as a tack, have never gotten a ticket."

"Well, I don't know. The day turns are filled. You got any experience?"

"Yes, but not with cab driving specifically." He smiled. "I got this map, though, so I'm ready to go. Been studying the layout of the city. Go on, ask me a question."

"Well, now, that's good. What brings you to Ft. Collins?"

"I want to learn the trade. I've been working construction down in Denver. Too seasonal. This seems like a job I could enjoy. You get to meet a lot of people, serve little old ladies. That's important to me."

"A religious fellow, eh? Mormon?" he asked, looking around to an older woman on a couch who'd just come out of the john. She was smoking a Camel.

There were mops and brooms in the far-right hand corner. A refrigerator along the right wall, some stacked tires, minimal tread, between it and the Coke machine. Old socks, just under the couch, and a huge map on the left wall.

There were maps all over that wall for that matter, some with pins in them. Ft. Collins, Loveland, Laporte, Greeley, Estes Park. Little reminders about timetables, when the vans got in from Stapleton, flat fare rates for long trips were taped up here and there as well, some on the wide window in front of them.

"Come on, John, give the guy a chance," the woman said, winking at me. "Sounds like a company man to me."

"Well, we might be able to use you at nights, at least to start with. 30% and tips, that's what we pay. Interested?" You can start tonight. I can get some sleep. . . . What kind of work did you say you've been doing?" Then he quickly added, "Do you have any references? I need dependability around here."

"I'll take it . . . insurance work. Besides, I like people, face to face stuff, you know?"

"John, it's 33%," the lady threw in.

"Okay. What'd I say, 30%? My mistake. . . . You can sleep on the couch. Look, we've got a nice refrigerator. You can put your lunch in here. . . . What we got in here anyway? . . . Whoa, look at this!" he said pulling out a brown bag. "I bet there's some sandwiches in here."

"John, that's my lunch."

"I know, Mary. But sharing is sharing. Ain't that what the Good Book says. . . . What was your name?"

"James, James Bailey."

"James. That's a book in the Bible. That's what the Bible says, isn't it? Look, egg salad. Oh, I love egg salad. My favorite. Mary, how could you have known that was my favorite? How could you have known that?"

"Oh, take the damned thing. John, I swear you squeeze every nickel till the buffalo dies." He took that, I could see, as a compliment, ate the sandwich with all the slow joy of a gourmand, his feet up, thanking her repeatedly for it.

"Mary, you're a very generous woman, very generous."

Soon it became apparent, however, even to him, that she was not going to respond positively, so he began to sport a hurt look. "Mary, you're not sore, are you? Why, after all I've done for you? . . . But, here, let me make it up to you." And with that he unlocked the Coke machine: one for each of us.

"Okay, James. We'll see you tonight at about eleven, then. The couch will be all yours," he said after a few more moments of talk. Then he remembered he hadn't shown me anything yet, so he proceeded to run down what I would need to know as Mary took over the mike. I needed to learn how to use the pager, so I wouldn't miss calls if I were out driving.

Welcome to small city taxi life.

It was a good six months; weird, but good, a real baptism. Border-line psychotics, a crook and his girlfriend, running out of the cab, across a field when they got onto the coded messages I kept getting from the dispatcher. 10-99, 10-99. (Real subterfuge there.) Once I actually had to wait in the cab while a passenger got out, left his door open as he walked up to meet some guy on a porch off the frontage road, decked him. Then he walked back, calm as the spring night, told me the guy owed him five grand. (He asked me not to tell the cops where I'd dropped him.) Another guy, an heir to the western painter Remington, got so giddy after a meeting with family lawyers, that he actually insisted on buying me a new car.

I still wonder why I said no. (Think I was worried about taxes).

One guy had me take him forty-five miles, up to the VA in Cheyenne. A real paranoiac, he stayed in my rear view mirror, trying to work through his issues. He did end up giving me a $24 tip. (Several days later I read about him in a Boulder paper.)

You try to be there as best you can.

(At that point my Beat poems took on some of the character of C. K. Williams and Nicanor Parra – the latter's anti-poetry. Influences from Rill's grad school.)

The Edges of Mercy

Colorado blue, small city taxi days:
glacial flows on the north sides of houses,
streets, snow-filled early,
wet and steaming in the afternoon sun;
this guy I was taking to the VA in Cheyenne,
all over the back seat mirror,
talking to himself, to me:
"So are you going to turn me in,
or *what?*"

(Days later he stabbed someone in a Boulder bar.)

Another guy, still in Nam, wore a neck brace,
was, like his woman who never disguised
her hatred of him, as blonde and tan
as he wanted to be.
He *knew* how much his voice grated,
that was the thing that got me:
the fraying twine of it when we were alone,
pieces of his cracked will
all over the back seat. And he wouldn't let up.
He'd talk, just so I could hear the bodies of the dead
bob up, bloat in the Mekong Delta.
I felt like Sartre in hell, the meter exacting
just how much time I had to pay
as I drove him to liquor stores, Denny's,
to late night construction sites:
looking for parties which never materialized.

There was this Chicano, too, who'd be lit every morning,
going to or coming from the bar, his mother's house.
He'd dig out his belches with a ritualized hand,
fisting at the waist.

"I was born naked," he's say.
"Now I've got a pair of pants.
Fuck the parade."

But I could write poems, too,
cruise down wide streets, grassy divides,
felt like Rockefeller in my old clothes.
I could ride the Overland Trail next to mountains,
pick up some guy out there
who'd be cursing, screen door and his woman,
banging behind him, a couple of Colorado chickens
squawking in his wake.

None of it ever got any of us home, of course,
each of us wanting our lives so badly
that they fed on everything else,
the stuff of repentance, praise finally,
if you choose to see it that way:
a hundred reasons daily to pick your feet up,
a hundred reasons to put them down again –
wearing out the soles of your traveling shoes.

We had to buy booze for people who didn't feel like leaving their dark trailers. It was sad, though most were nice enough folk. But there were regulars, too, and they could be fun. There was this one little Mexican guy, with a mostly toothless grin. I could never understand his attempts at English, and of course, I had no Spanish. We got on well, though, me with my leaning questions, him with his willing and happy nods, gestures. I'd take him and his groceries into his little shack on the run-down north side of town. John called him "the pickle man" because he'd worked for 40 years making them.

There was a close shave with a nice-looking trailer park woman.

I wanted her, couldn't.

A young Japanese woman came later, though she did not want me to meet any of her family. (Couldn't blame her there!)

I liked sticking my old boots out the Checker windows during down times, worked on poems. Rill was always willing to look at them. The sky always seemed so blue out west – though I never did find any Beats.

It wasn't all sunshine, though.

Evil was (and is) real.

One morning, alone – my mates, out of town, I roused, feeling an ugly, weighted presence lying on top of my chest (after a borderline-conscious fantasy or two). This happened before sleep had completely passed, just before I found myself totally awake. The creature, as it turned out, was like Gollum or Wormwood: a spirit who connived through and despite my near attention.

It wanted me to say yes to it, to any of a wild array of partners, scenes.

I caught on, and though part of me wanted something of what he had to offer, the other, slightly better part, tried to pull away.

I prayed, worked to form words (I was impeded), put up a fight.

That paltry resistance must've irritated Screwtape, because he stepped back to allow a larger, more ancient force to have a go: a more menacing presence. He, too, lay on top of me (though he had no form), covered my body, sneered at my weakness.

He tried to cow, devour.

I could feel the timeless history of the thing, its long rage. The creature was strong enough to rip the head off of my body (to piss down my throat).

He breathed, spiritually, on me, mocking my small-time frame, nature. He demanded that I give him what he already possessed: power, a throne in my pathetic life. He could make things happen. . . . I would pay less if I said yes.

I prayed (weakly) harder, as the thing tried to spiritually suffocate me. I fought to move my mouth, to utter, get the words out, to say a rosary, even as my bed seemed to creak with his dense weight, hatred.

He was not impressed.

I'd seen my enemy. Too powerful for me.

No angels came to comfort, but the prayers did eventually work, or draw enough of a response to save my hide. And then, two weeks later, I came across Malachi Martin's *Hostage to the Devil*, and saw how, in each possession case, the victim had to say yes before the devil could have his instrument.

Charming. (The bigger the fool, the bigger the fool.)

These days I drive in Cleveland, part-time.

As God's will would have it, about a year after the move, I picked up a surprised Periwinkle at the airport. (Shocked me, too.) We did an evening out once she'd cleared her schedule. We shot hoops in a drizzle (something she would do so later while massively pregnant), shared beers and crab legs under a wet tree, plastic hats. (She had an extra one.) I was surprised and delighted by how in control of her life she seemed.

She liked my little apartment on West 27th, out near the Cleveland Zoo.

You see all kinds of weird stuff driving cab in a city. I've run into domestic scenes: gun shots, smashed TV screens, women holding their bloody heads in their hands, the sounds of heavy feet, children screaming upstairs, cops standing (clueless) right next to me in the living room. The Tuesday before I picked up Periwinkle, a gay ex-Gospel singer broke down in the back seat of my cab, crying from loneliness. We sat with the meter off, talked frankly about who Jesus is, something I rarely get a chance to do. Finally, I prayed over him, gave him a few addresses.

Hope he prays for me.

I still try to love, lift up my fares, but I fall short. (Judgment comes so naturally!) It's amazing, how completely I've got to change. I have to move beyond my obsession – me. Sometimes I feel the grace I walk in; I can enter into the chapel of the moment. But those times don't last.

When I first came back to Cleveland, I spent some time in a few small monasteries. I started driving cab (my wagon full of sunflowers), as I'd planned, had even gotten an MA at Cleveland State (Yeats). I did grad school assistant work in comp, and taught as an adjunct at a local community college. (Some lady did a piece on me and my first little local book, *The Sandaled Foot*, for *Cleveland Magazine* – "The Beat Monastic Cabbie.")

I managed to keep my Yellow Checker thing going, despite the fact that ridership in general declined. Between '70-'76, the number of cab drivers dropped from 1500 to 761. By '87, the city canceled the monopoly, and by '93, we were leasing.

Divine Mercy intervened.

A Denver lawyer sent me Amelia's papers, a nice little chunk of change – and some surprising news. Jesus, the God of diversity, allowed me to see that I'm one-half Choctaw.

Thank You, Jesus, for my heritage, and for the whole state of Mississippi (and Oklahoma)! As heaven would have it, a full-time position opened up on the eastern campus of Cuyahoga Community College.

(I was tempted to show up for my interview in breech cloth.)

I was married by then, had a beautiful son, so I grabbed the affirmation offer (my teaching numbers were high) and ran with it like a hungry Native prairie dog.

I thank the Chahta spirit and, through the years, have tried to be faithful to that part of me.

The students over the decades have been a joy: nobody in junior college drives daddy's car. I still see them, young and old, all over the place in Cleveland, in malls, at Guard's games, along the lake; get invited to old writing group get-togethers now and then. (We had very good lit. mages. over at CCC East: *Black Ascensions, Breakwall*.) I still publish as I go, though more slowly as I've embraced this retirement thing. Books have come, four hundred and fifty poems or so in little magazines and dead presses. Local publishers have been generous: the Cleveland State University Poetry Center, Falling Down Press, Pranayama, Burning Press. Out-of-state ones as well: Kaufmann, CMJ, Wipf & Stock, Angelico.

Two interviews on WVIZ, the local educational TV outlet.

An NPR thing. (Warhol's fifteen minutes.)

I do fewer readings these days, which is just as well. So many of the old spots are gone: Genesis, The Rascal House, and Bobbie McGee's on Euclid. We'd sometimes invite local street friends, devoted to the grape, set them up in the back or front rows. They were always good for inappropriate (and therefore necessary) commentary, dialogue. Some of those widened nights ended up in weird Odyssean swales and troughs, wine-dark stars above.

The Cleveland Heights Library, Coventry Yard were nice, Mac's Backs. Low-impact people, as an old Colorado State python-owning student-friend of mine would have put it.

I've co-edited a few Christian anthologies, and so have met a bunch of national poet friends, too, of one stripe or another, not all of them Beat or landed-gentry Catholics: William Stafford and Denise Levertov, Franz Wright (great fun there: he and Liz came in for a reading, wanted my wife and I to adopt them before they left), Tom Andrews, Scott Cairns, Syd Lea (who absolutely killed it with my students), Paul Mariani, Sophia Starnes, Angela O'Donnell, Dana Gioia, Marjorie Maddox; Don Richmond, who introduced me to Rowan Williams, the Archbishop of Canterbury.

I've learned a lot from poets, both contemporary and not. Yeats. No surprise, there. Kavanagh's Catholic heart. Mistral's emotional power. But the most crucial changes have come from elsewhere. Once I decided to give Jesus-God the primary focus He has always asked for in my life and work, I began to find poetry writing a powerful, prayerful process through which I could open myself up to the mystery of His Being, to heaven, literally. This has been true in both invention and in revision. (Merton says as much in his first New Directions *Selected*, "Poetry is contemplation.") It's certainly how Jesus-God most clearly reveals Himself to me.

We wait. He responds.

It's how all art works, really.

I hold out for that, for the "No, not I, but Christ," who I want to live within me. Poetry-writing, when seen this way, literally becomes a demand for the new. I would tell my secular students as much (using different words). If I know what's coming next in the poem, I stop. I need to be surprised. After all, how can I allow Jesus to say the new thing unless I hold out for it? God will surprise us for each second of eternity.

I just need the courage to wait for heaven.

I am convinced that we should be able to write original poems until the day we die (or until He pulls the plug). Mostly I do Bly-like ghazals these days (see opening poem), praise poems adopted from the Muslims. The form is helpful, blank verse, six stanzas; it insists that I get help in filling it out.

All this is a nice way to strive for humility. That and wisdom are the things I always pray for.

Which brings me to the weirdest moment, a gift not asked for. A few years ago, I had been praying, pleading for those two things: humility (sanity) and wisdom, when suddenly, the Holy Spirit powerfully broke in.

These things happen every once in a while for most Christians, I would think.

(Similar experiences had occurred to me. Years ago, for example, while I was sitting in my living room on 1411 Ridge Road, Milton revealed himself in spirit. He simply walked across my living room. I told my wife, who was in the kitchen, chopping onions, but there was really nothing she could do about that. Another time, much later, St. Anthony likewise took a stroll, this time right next to me in St. Peter's Adoration chapel. Oddly enough—he was sporting a beard. And then of course there are dreams – old men dream them, which allow for all sorts of messages and messengers: Thomas Merton, Catherine Doherty, and Pope Francis (for a four-hour visit). One time Padre Pio came, impatient with me because I had asked to see him. I just thought it would be cool. He had more important things to do!)

Anyway, the Holy Spirit-humility thing felt like some spiritual window breaking. God told me (without words) that since I had not prayed for fame or wealth, that he would bless these poems.

I hoped, later, that more readers would happen during my lifetime, but now I don't think that is likely, which makes sense. Our lives, after all, are about Jesus, not about us. The lives of great recent saints like both Faustina and her Jesuit spiritual director ran in this same "later" kind of river. Neither lived to see their work completed, so why should we lessers? The drama that matters is not about us. It's only right that we should leave before things happen.

(The tendency to claim trophies for ourselves is strong.)

Let Him have all the glory. He certainly deserves it.

I kept a small crucifix in my office for years – got away with it because I also had a nice fat little Buddha in there to keep me company, a menorah as well; and bigger than all of those – a framed picture of the WWI Choctaw code talkers, two oversized ceramic ceremonious green ears of our corn; a stack of the DVD Vision Quest on a table nearby as well.

The idea was that everybody has to follow his or her own path.

Because that's how it is.

Christianity always contains multitudes (most of them believers).

So the world hasn't beaten a track to my door, at least in any big way. I've won a Fabilli, a Körte, an OAC grant – résumé available upon request! Besides, the world is mostly anti-climax, anyway, isn't it? Any success we experience is always dwarfed by the Monday mornings and people that follow.

Family life's been good. (The best of that comes across in the poetry.) Most of my sin goes there: spiritual whining, impulse control – big surprise there, and self-appointed adjudication. (I keep a white wig in my closet.)

Periwinkle teaches art to Catholic high school girls. We've had three kids, four grand-kids now! Ha. Who'd a seen that coming? We've done some traveling: Sagrada Familia in Barcelona, those curved Dome steps inside the Vatican – I hate heights, couldn't make it all the way to the top. Prague ("The Friary" restaurant), JP II's Poland, Ireland, Glasgow (to see a fan), Japan (for a haiku contest).

When we were younger, we canoed once down the Amazon, tried skydiving.

She became an acupuncturist for a season, sold homeopathic medicines.

Sill serves as a reader at Church.

What does it all mean, what has it ever meant?

It means that Jesus-God is still on His burnished throne of praise (our bodies, our voices, our minds and all matter rooted and moving in Him). It means that the future is bright, and mine – yours.

Some reap, others sow.

At any rate, He still apparently thinks I am a good idea.

My dear Spiritual Director, Fr. Pelton (*Circling the Sun: Meditations on Christ in Liturgy and Time*), has recently passed, though I know he's here with me. Life flies by, but you get to hold it some nights – your dear wife's face in your hands.

I want to dance into my death/birth with St. Anthony when the time comes, a new poem in each fist.

As Fr. Bob would say, "It's all Nazareth."

The important thing is that it all matters.

Periwinkle has been the focal point. No denouement there, though other people have certainly blessed me, too. Over at Mac's Backs on Coventry after I did a reading, I met both Bill Thomas and Mark Steeve, one a Catholic, one an ex-. (They didn't know each other.) Bill had gotten his PhD late from Case, is a white male who wouldn't do research and so couldn't find tenure-track work. He doesn't care, though. Not really. He'd worked for years as an engineer, owns his house out in Sagamore Hills. So he's sitting on some money.

Life of Riley – for a while anyway.

Recently, it's pulmonary fibrosis, a breathing machine. (Smoker.)

He likes talking Neihbur, Dillard, Emerson, Rahner and a happy death. He's always on to something new in physics, theology. We used to do Chief Wahoo, bookstores. He taught part time for years over at CSU, would occasionally bring me in as guest poet.

Mark owned one of those bookstores. He pitched on a softball team, roped me in to that. A low-rent, tweed-jacket kind of guy, whatever his successes; he dressed in grungy corduroy sport coats, patches at the elbow, jeans, sold semi-squalid cartoon collections from beneath his counter, as well as fine old editions of the classics.

He'd sit in state, in a nice old swivel wooden chair. I would come in and we would talk things over. It was his East 6th Street domain, him with balding pate and ponytail, talking Larry Flynt and *Hustler*, the Indians, or Catholic-y poets: Mary Karr, Kate Daniels, Ernesto Cardenal – an ex-Merton postulant, Minister of Nicaraguan Culture. . . . The United Fruit Company! (Saw the latter read once in Pittsburgh with Scott Cairns. All he wanted to talk about was extraterrestrials, *Star Trek*, and new contemplative communities.)

Mark still knows where you can get the best Korean food in town – insists (correctly) that I have a permanent acid hang-over.

I love him dearly.

He works out of his home these days, after a down-turn, is a good straight-forward kind of guy. He's actually broken out his catcher's mitt on his side street once or twice to get a look at my knuckleball.

He got married, but then his wife went to India.

Her daughter, step-daughter, still lives in the house with him. Nothing untoward, just odd. It's all wonderful in its way.

The greatest blessing, of course, has been Periwinkle.

Once she became a Catholic, an old friend, we slowly seemed to find time for each other. Occasionally, we'd rent dirt bikes and ride them over the bridal paths through the Metroparks — until Ranger Rick read us the riot act.

So we took to taking walks down around Tinker's Creek, near where she grew up, or over on the West Side, in Berea. On one particular pilgrimage, in the middle of an intensely illumined spiritual talk, over near BW, two squirrels came over to my feet, actually took the acorns I offered. It was odd. Small creatures (and babies) usually retreated whenever I approached back then. But this whole time was different. God was present in a very powerful, almost Pentecostal Franciscan way.

We couldn't deny it — the spirit was strong just then on the two of us; we smiled to be in the middle of such heavenly companions. It washed the whole early green scene. The trees seemed to rise up around us, like hands in prayer, the slow shake; mottled shade, the spare growth underneath.

We were pleased to walk in the Spirit's presence, to talk about Jesus-God, the difficulties, about what He was doing in our lives, about what our lives were like before He came.

We both felt intensely cared for then, as if it were just us and Him.

Fine moments, and many more of them followed, enough to get us thinking.

Of course, one never plans a future around moments of graceful, illumined Presence (though that might not be a bad idea).

She was still going through her spiritual honeymoon phase at the time – every little prayer answered, or so it seemed to me, in the affirmative. I needed to wait until she came down before I could figure where we were at, though I enjoyed sharing in the obvious joy she expected would always be there.

I wondered what it'd be like when she finally did come down? The occasional neurosis, hers or mine, rubbing us down to our last nerves?

I still don't have an answer to most of those questions!

She likes to go where things are most real, on an edge, close enough to look down over the cliff's side. On some summer nights, trees above, we drive down in the flats in my cab. It's nice, breezy nights under a red light, the leafy speech of summer boughs above small bridges. (She pays the fare.) She's great company, the best I've known, still filled with the same childlike incredulity she's always had: with hops, wise retort. She does her "Direction for our Times" contemplative prayer rooms, tells me all about it – St. John of the Cross and Mary and Jesus in chaise lounges, talking things over with her.

(Sometimes I feel like I'm in the wrong Woody Allen prayer boxcar.)

She's playful in life and language, in sewing patterns, a fellow dark beer drinker. Even as we age, we still like to dangle our bare feet (sometimes with our grown up Down's son) over the concrete ledge down by the creek, talk Romano Guardini, poetry, painting, wait for and listen to baseball. She likes the language, all the numbers in sports: four to two in the tenth, the pitcher who just had a two-inning outing, or the entire bottom of the TV screen during a professional football game.

We've become more intimate over the years, as age begins to take us. My own gratitude has profoundly deepened. I mean, how can I adequately thank someone who's given me decades, someone who's been there through the holly, through my failures and wash-outs, someone who's shown me repeatedly where the real gift lies—in the decades given, an entire youth spent in learning to love a man who is largely a fool, sometimes by looking after him, crabby and home-bound, vomit-sick, sometimes by keeping vigil (along with the machines) at his hospital bedside? How could I possibly thank this woman for her unalloyed joy and play, for her patience in putting up with my debilitating neuroses, which can gouge like cut glass, neuroses which demand more attention than anyone could possibly give them, which often do not want to be appeased, defects which in some way only want to hurt, to pass along the pain?

That works both ways of course. It's how mercy works.

This is typical husband-wife fare. This is how we both learn to love. The other part is easy: our considerable gifts. We both can be pleasant company, witty, kind enough even to marry. But burdens must be borne, shouldered. That's why they call them crosses.

Each grisly adventure-episode passes, each trying intensity wanes, of course, (too gradually) along with the old us, as we work our way toward heaven. The holy friction continues to wear away our roughest edges, teaches us how to lay down our lives, to love. And more: it teaches me that the root problem here in every situation is not my wife, never my wife. It is always me. Growth is about how I respond—to what doesn't matter so much.

Jesus allows trials because I am slower than I would have thought possible. (The adolescent—infant in me sometimes—dies too slowly, breaking things along the way.)

Life is always about the person next to us, their childhood, isn't it? They wail, out of proportion to the situation. So we love, are called to do so as best we can. Once one's been married long enough, he knows that the familiar difficulty at hand will more than likely pass, because Jesus, he's come to see, is behind this pilgrimage, literally minute by minute, second by second. He has always been so.

What is good endures—moves the furniture.

Periwinkle has always been an artist, a childlike joy. She delightfully plays a beautiful home-spun classical piano. She's mothered with an, at times, overly anxious heart, but she also gives much more to the poor than I ever would have. As I say, she has endured both my silences and occasional sullenness, my unspoken cave-ins.

In fact, she's growing into a small saint precisely because she has endured.

She often takes the lead in our domestic church because she can love more heroically than I can. This ability, I've come to be convinced, has been fostered by her ability to carry and deliver children. Like all mothers, she has literally given up her body for nine months at a time to another human being, in her case, three times. This is a cross no man can duplicate. Because of this fact, women simply know how to love more deeply than men can.

But there is more mercy.

The years of fighting her own first family psychological battles have deepened her as well, given her an ability to respond lovingly to people: to the lady next to her or to a cashier in the supermarket line, or last week, to a stranger's child at a summer music outing who needed mosquito ointment. Borders are for other people. Like heaven, she will not be bound. She reaches out because the mercy of Jesus has been imprinted so deeply inside her. His long, continual free gift is still changing her—and us because of that.

She has often become Jesus, embodying the joyful sacrifice which is always, in her merciful heart, complete. Because of this fact, she knows me, covers me, has nurtured me in ways only those deeply in love with Him can know about.

She tells me I do the same for her. But it's hard to see much of that in yourself.

She's become progressively sweeter, more complete as the years roll by.

On a good day, it can feel as if she's been dipped in some kind of spiritual honey.

204

(She's been in that abused skin for the long haul.)

Whatever I had to endure growing up – two missing parents – is dwarfed by her past. Most of us do not recover completely, I think. And this serves God, and us. We need to stay aware of our flaws, baggage. It makes love real.

The damage we've both had to deal with has, unfortunately, also in some small way affected our children. Parents everywhere try to break whatever harmful cycle they've been part of. They try to move beyond their forebears. But they cannot – not completely. The two of us have, like it or not, weighted our children with some of our baggage because we have not loved well enough, because we've learned to manage our sins and inclinations too slowly. It would be nice if the only negative thing I ever gave my children was original sin.

We have to ask for forgiveness often.

This is the human condition. This is why we must beg for His mercy, humility.

We learn that He is big enough, covers every sin, knows the weaknesses which give rise to them. (And He likes us.)

Periwinkle and I, we walk together, two fools – in love with God, each other, to the extent that our crusty hearts allow. I love her in ways I never could have four decades ago. She has, as I've said, been a continual lesson for me. This is how I need to grow; this is how I need to love. Would I lay down my life for her? Maybe it's too easy to say I have, but something very much like that has occurred, in some small way. Will I pick up the garbage for her? With I help her wash and wax the car?

How many times, how far can I carry the garbage?

It all sounds dramatic, and it is; but I am thankful – and weak.

What we have in each other is what we have with every person we meet. I come with my weaknesses, my awkwardness, my wants. This is who I am before Jesus, before my fellow men and women. We both do this, try to, and so see the other more clearly. We are profoundly flawed followers of Jesus Christ, whom we love with all we can of what we are.

I am made whole here on this earth by her. She shows me how to proceed.

She does gallery shows all over this part of the country, down in Mexico once.

Our kids have grown up, having survived middle school, late-discovered autism, our parenting.

As they say in Byzantine Easter liturgies: "Christ is risen." "Truly, He is risen."

Tonight's a date night. We're going to a local art show. One of her former students. We'll talk about that, us, the kids. God will continue to transform us, as He's always done — without much knowledge on our parts.

We try to keep our oars in the water, to be ready to meet new Beat-like friends.

The open kind, those in the middle of things, without too many answers.

Mistral and Kavanagh!

Mercy.

ABOUT THE AUTHOR

DAVID CRAIG taught literature and creative writing at the Franciscan University of Steubenville for more than 30 years. These days he tries to sharpen what's left for him to do, serving his family, working poems, a novel. His wife, in the meantime, amid all of her interests (painting, sewing, classical piano), has surprisingly taken an interest in Stan Getz — whose music is currently playing in the kitchen.

Ingram Content Group UK Ltd.
Milton Keynes UK
UKHW012254080523
421436UK00015B/380/J